# How to
# HANG LOOSE
## in an
## Uptight World

# How to
# HANG LOOSE
## in an
# Uptight World

## Elizabeth Baker

**PELICAN PUBLISHING COMPANY**
Gretna 2002

The word "Pelican" and the depiction of a pelican are
trademarks of Pelican Publishing Company, Inc., and are
registered in the U.S. Patent and Trademark Office.

**Library of Congress Cataloging-in-Publication Data**

Baker, Elizabeth.
   How to hang loose in an uptight world /
Elizabeth Baker.
      p. cm.
   ISBN 1-58980-011-7 (pbk. : alk. paper)
      1. Stress management. 2. Stress (Psychology)
   3. Relaxation.  I. Title.

RA785 .B34 2002
155.9'042—dc21

2001059822

Printed in the United States of America
Published by Pelican Publishing Company, Inc.
1000 Burmaster Street, Gretna, Louisiana 70053

# Contents

Chapter One        Hassles, Problems, and Pressures . . . . . . 7

Chapter Two        Measuring Your Personal
                   Stress Level  . . . . . . . . . . . . . . . . . . . 17

Chapter Three      Choices: The Key to Lower Stress . . . . 30

Chapter Four       Stress Busters: No Time Required . . . . 41

Chapter Five       Stress Busters: One to
                   Fifteen Minutes. . . . . . . . . . . . . . . . . 51

Chapter Six        Stress Busters: Thirty Minutes
                   to Two Hours . . . . . . . . . . . . . . . . . . 64

Chapter Seven      Stress Busters: Twenty-Four
                   to Seventy-Two Hours  . . . . . . . . . . . 73

Chapter Eight      Faith: The Ultimate Answer
                   to Stress . . . . . . . . . . . . . . . . . . . . . 89

                   Appendix I. . . . . . . . . . . . . . . . . . . . . 99

                   Appendix II . . . . . . . . . . . . . . . . . . . 104

                   Notes . . . . . . . . . . . . . . . . . . . . . . . 109

# CHAPTER 1

# Hassles, Problems, and Pressures

When I talk to clients in my counseling office about stress, they often discount my advice. Sure, stress plays a part in their damaged relationships and damaged bodies, but so what? They think stress is like the weather—something people talk about but are helpless to change—and a peaceful lifestyle became extinct somewhere between "Little House On the Prairie" and "Happy Days."

They would love to go back to the time before beepers and cell phones and rush-hour traffic, but the idea is impractical. Somewhere back in history they might have had to face an occasional bear, but at least there would have been no soccer practice, carpools, and problems with the Internal Revenue Service. However, the truth is that even a time machine could not guarantee a stress-free lifestyle. Hassles, problems, and pressures have always been part of the human experience.

My grandma was a woman under pressure. She married late in life and started her family just in time for the Great Depression. Since Grandpa was a sharecropper, they were the poorest of the poor. With little education, limited job skills, and five little girls to rear, her choices were very few. At times starvation was a real possibility.

Wealthier farmers in those days grew large fields of blackeyed peas. Those were the days before chemical fertilizers, and the peas were plowed under in the fall in an effort to enrich the soil.

One such farmer lived near Grandma's family, and he offered to let her glean the peas before the crop was turned under. The whole family worked from dawn 'til night securing every pea and drying them. That winter the peas comprised 90 percent of the family diet and they were eaten every day for months.

It was not only poverty that challenged Grandma. The physical work and time pressures were constant. Planting and harvesting have deadlines assigned by nature that are just as strict as anything invented by corporate America. In addition, there was an urgency in every job assigned her. Such tasks as sewing dresses out of feed sacks and making lye soap in a kettle over a fire in the yard were not optional adventures but necessary items filling her "in-basket." Grandma and Grandpa were a godly pair and they raised their children well, but they lived and died under pressure and were intimately acquainted with stress.

The only thing that has changed since Grandma's day is that we now have a word for the struggle of life. We call it STRESS. It is a word Grandma never used because it was not even invented until shortly before 1956. Today, we can measure it, scientifically examine it, and prescribe drugs when our bodies start wearing down under the weight of it. But, like a raging epidemic with no cure, most of us believe we can't do anything substantial to *prevent* it.

The good news is that this belief is wrong. We *can* do something about stress. And the best news of all is that we can do it without taking a time machine back to Walnut Creek or trading our cell phones for butter churns.

In this short, easy-to-read book, I promise to teach you how to cope with stress and how to do it without significantly disrupting your modern lifestyle. I will show you fifteen stress-busting ideas divided into digestible bites. Selecting a couple of these ideas and following them for three weeks can impact both the quality and the length of your life on earth. We will discuss these ideas in detail in the next few chapters, and all fifteen are listed in abbreviated form in Appendix I.

However, before you race on to the Appendix in an effort to defeat stress instantly, you will do yourself a favor if you read through the next two chapters so you can understand the dynamics of stress and how it has impacted your personal life. An enemy with an unknown face has a distinct advantage.

Learning a little about stress will become a major asset in your efforts to defeat it. So slow down and read the next two chapters at your leisure. I guarantee the knowledge you gain will be worth it. Then, adapt the suggested stress busters to your personal schedule and needs. In twenty-one days you will be well on your way to peace.

## THE STORY OF STRESS

Much of what we know about stress and how to cope with it can be credited to one man, Hans Selye. In 1925 Hans was a first-year medical student at the University of Prague. The troubled political times had pushed academia to allow students to enter the medical programs as quickly as they could pass the necessary exams. Hans was only nineteen when he attended his first medical lecture. He was starry-eyed enough to believe that any question could be answered if proper methods of research were applied and young enough to not be contaminated by the medical biases of the older generation.

The thing that struck Hans from the very beginning was the strange way that his teachers seemed to seek solutions for specific diseases and symptoms, yet paid little or no attention to the general idea of just being sick. Often he would be told that while a patient might be achy, feverish, somewhat nauseated, and generally not feeling well, the attending physician should wait until more specific symptoms developed before attempting treatment. Only when a specific disease was identified could intervention be applied.

Hans could not understand why a doctor should wait. Of course there must be a specific disease for a specific treatment to be applied, but should not the medical establishment want to study sickness in general? Why did sickness itself exist? What was its process?

He would later express his amazement by writing, "Surely, if it is important to find remedies which help against one disease or another, it would be even more important to learn something about the mechanism of being sick and the means of treating this 'general syndrome of sickness, which [is] apparently super-imposed upon all individual diseases!"[1]

Hans' desire to understand sickness in general rather than any disease in particular was laughed at by his professors. It was self-evident that people who were sick would look and feel sick. They assured him that there was no common thread among the many various diseases, and if there was, it would never be found. Hans accepted the evaluation of his professors and tried to forget about it, but in the back of his mind remained a simmering question: Why not study the general process of all disease? It would be another ten years before Hans took up the question for serious study.

Shortly after World War II, Hans immigrated to Canada, where he was employed as a young research assistant in the biochemistry department of McGill University in Montreal. It was here that Hans once again took up the study of sickness in general. He felt that studying the general way the body adapted itself to various demands would eventually lead to a way to prevent disease from getting a foothold, thus curing the patient long before specific symptoms began to appear.

Like many scientific discoveries, Hans' work was helped forward by a fortunate accident that enabled him to devise specific experiments which put his ideas to the test. Hans had asked a new lab assistant to give injections to several dozen white rats, but the assistant accidentally failed to place the needle deeply enough. When Hans returned to the lab, he found several dozen rats with pockets of air on their backs. These large bubbles were located between the skin and the underlying tissues. When his anger cooled, Hans realized that he could use the pockets of air to take his study to the next level.[2]

Dr. Selye designed a set of experiments around rats with pockets on their backs. He was sure that he could demonstrate to a skeptical medical community that the bodies of all animals had certain general responses to any kind of sickness or injury. These general responses came before a specific illness could be identified and were always a precursor to it. He believed that the future of medicine would be in controlling and treating these underlying general responses rather than waiting for specific illnesses to become fully active. Seyle's experiments were detailed, very controlled, and strictly scientific.

Hans filled the air pockets on the backs of his rats with various irritants, thus creating an injury against which the body of each rat would have to fight. Every rat would be working in exactly the same way trying to rid himself of exactly the same amount of trouble, and if the irritant was mild, it was logical that each rat would recover. Then he introduced another element to half of his carefully matched rats, thus creating two groups. That element was what he would later call *stress*.

Part of the rats were allowed to rest while the remainder were forced to adapt to various difficult circumstances, such as limited foods, strenuous exercise, cold, heat, or psychological[3] strain. These difficult circumstances were, of course, hard on the rats. However, they did not have any *direct* bearing on the injury each rat carried equally on his back.

In one of his early experiments, Selye injected the air pockets on several dozen of his rats with a mild irritant. He let half the rats rest while the other half were subjected to stresses. Surprisingly, the stressed rats got well faster than the ones who were allowed to rest. Hard work had cured them!

In his next experiment the rats were injected with a stronger irritant, and again half of them were stressed while the other half rested. The results were the exact opposite of previous experiments. This time, the stressed rats died and the rested ones slowly got well. Hard work had killed them!

In both of these experiments, it was not the irritant in the back pocket that killed the rats. The injury had not been enough to cause death. Also, it was not the stress that killed the rats. Stress alone would not have been enough to cause death. Something happened inside the body of each rat. There was some kind of response process that was reacting to both the injury and the other stressors. Somehow the body was combining these responses and the internal systems were being overwhelmed as they tried to fight on both fronts.

As he watched his rats and carefully documented their progress, Hans proved that difficult circumstances that had no direct bearing on the original injury could impact the healing process. It did not matter what the difficult circumstance was, just so long as it took energy.

This new approach to study needed new words to describe the process. Hans coined the word *stress* to describe the process of adaptation and *stressor* to identify any substance or situation that put the process in motion. Because the stressors were general and could come from any source—heat, cold, physical injury, psychological strain—he gave stress the official title of *general adaptation syndrome.*

In time, Hans was able to isolate the three organs that were always affected when a body was forced to adapt to difficult circumstance. They were the (1) stomach, (2) adrenal glands, and (3) thymus/lymph nodes. These three sets of organs were always affected in the same way and always produced the same results: illness.

It did not matter what stressor had been used, and it did not matter what animal was involved in the experiments. The results were the same whether the subject was a rat dealing with excessive exercise or the CEO of a major corporation dealing with a union strike.

When the energy required for adapting to difficult circumstances lasted long enough, or when it was severe enough, symptoms of disease would appear in these three organs. In time, specific signs of illness came as the body began to break down at the weakest link. If the demand was not released, disease would progress and the organism would die.

Hans knew he had found what he had been seeking for so long. He had found a syndrome of body responses that *preceded* specific disease symptoms. For the first time in human history a scientist was not studying a specific disease, but rather a precursor to all diseases.

## A PERSONAL NOTE

Invariably, after I have given a lecture on stress, someone will come up and ask about my personal lifestyle. Fair enough. I would not give money to a financial agent who had just declared bankruptcy, and I can't expect readers to trust me unless I have successfully dealt with stress in my own life. Therefore I offer the following personal glimpse.

About eight years ago I went through a trauma that some call "burnout" or "hitting the wall." I was horrified and amazed that someone still in her forties could feel so bad for so long and still be functioning. My family physician said I had "chronic fatigue syndrome." I had never heard of it. The problem is much more understood now, but in the early nineties it was a mystery to most people and hotly debated even by those who believed it existed.[4]

It did not take long for me to give up on the medical establishment, but that did little to relieve my symptoms. Some days were better and some were worse, but the evening that it took both hands on the stair rail to pull myself up to my apartment I knew I was in deep trouble. I threw myself on the sofa and had to rest for ten minutes before I had energy enough to take off my coat.

Because this is not an autobiography, I won't go into detail about my ailments and my journey back to health. It is sufficient to say that the road involved learning about nutrition, rest, and time, and learning to invest more of myself in relating to others. It was also the beginning of my journey toward learning about stress and how it impacts the body.

Now I am in my late fifties and feel better than I have in years. I recently completed my doctor of philosophy degree, or

Ph.D. Anyone who has been involved in a program such as this knows how much pressure and work are involved. This particular degree required professionals to be working in their field before they were admitted to the program.[5]

When the day of graduation came at last, several of us were gathered for the event, and a colloquy was conducted to evaluate the experience. We went around the room sharing our personal stories and telling what the past few years had been like. I was surprised to hear what the others had gone through during the dissertation process.

One man got up at four o'clock each morning, worked until 6:30, then went to his job. Like mine, his profession was that of a counselor. He worked eight hours at the clinic. Then immediately upon returning home he ate a quick supper and saw clients in private practice until ten each night.

Another student said she had worked each night until three in the morning, then got up at seven to go to work. The rest of the students had followed a similar routine. When it came my turn to speak, I felt apologetic. I had slept eight to nine hours each night, and until the last few weeks of the program I always took at least a twenty-four-hour rest during the week.

But as I reconsidered the situation, my slight embarrassment faded. I had carried a full-time job as a counselor, written one of the books I used in the teaching practicum, completed a dissertation on philosophical anthropology, and finished the program in just over two and a half years. Since the program required a minimum of three years, I had to petition the graduate committee to be allowed early graduation.

I enjoyed several benefits that helped make early graduation possible, but I suspect the primary edge was that I got a full night's sleep each night and I occasionally took specific time to rest during stretches of peak stress. I had learned the hard way that burning the candle at both ends gives only a short-term increase in light. Ultimately, it just produces more ash than anything else.

Today, I don't perfectly practice what I teach, but I know that unless I am willing to rein in my strong type-A temperament and deal with the physical realities of my limitations, a very real and unmovable wall is waiting around the bend. Pushing myself until I hit that wall is not only unwise. In the end, it is unprofitable.

Realizing our limitations and maximizing our strengths is what stress management is all about. We must leave the rat race to the rats. Instead, we carve out times of rest for our bodies and practice times of peace for our souls. That is what I hope this book can help you accomplish.

## HOW TO USE THIS BOOK

This book contains eight chapters. You are just finishing Chapter 1, where, hopefully, I have convinced you that managing your stress **is** possible. In Chapter 2 you will understand more about stress and be given an opportunity to measure the impact it may be having on your body. In Chapter 3 you will be introduced to the most fundamental process of all stress reduction: choice.

Chapters 4, 5, 6, and 7 form a set of specific stress-reduction ideas, and the information is divided according to how much time it takes to implement each of these stress busters. There are fifteen ideas ranging from those that require no time commitment at all to a few that will involve a change in your basic lifestyle.

Don't worry. No one is expected to implement fifteen ideas! The number and variety of these stress-busting ideas is so that you can choose among them and find one or two that fit your lifestyle and personal need. I suggest that you never choose more than two ideas. It is far better to choose one or two doable things that you actually implement than to make a checklist of five and wear yourself our trying to relax!

The last chapter is a reality check. Life is hard, and reading this book will not change that fact. Some illnesses have no cure. Some problems have no solutions. However, even in those realities there is hope. Faith is the final solution and the ultimate answer to stress. Knowing what we believe and why we believe it will add to our peace and maximize our years on earth.

The last portion of this book contains two appendices. Appendix I lists all fifteen stress-busting ideas and gives a brief synopsis of each. Page numbers are given so you can quickly cross reference any idea for which you want more detailed description. However, I urge you to resist the temptation to turn to Appendix I now, assume you understand a few concepts, and immediately embark on a twenty-one-day trial.

Such action is possible, but it is not likely to be successful. After all, the whole idea of stress reduction is to slow down life. It is not to pack more into each day and do it more quickly than before. Racing to the Appendix would likely undermine the very purpose you are hoping to achieve!

Appendix II is specifically designed for those of the Christian and Jewish faiths. A list of fifteen passages from both the Old and New Testaments is given, and from the Old Testament the Hebrew names for God are listed. These lists provide an easy reference for meditation exercises.

I don't know if there ever has been a time when the life depicted in a Kincade painting or a peaceful place like Walnut Grove really existed. Somehow, I doubt it. But I do know that Jesus told His disciples that peace would be His parting gift to them.[6] It is a shame when we fill our world with schedules and pressures and the gift slips away.

# CHAPTER 2

# Measuring Your
# Personal Stress Level

It can be tempting to put stress reduction in the same category as most of our dieting attempts: a thing we seriously intend to do. Later. When things slow down a bit. However, there is one drawback to that approach. Stress kills people. Lots of them. It could kill you.

Because unrelenting stress is a precursor to disease, not a disease in itself, it can be easy to ignore. We live as though we were racing cars constantly running at full throttle. Then, when the head gasket blows, we blame the gasket, never considering that if we had slowed for a little maintenance now and then, the gasket might have lasted another 100,000 miles. When full-blown disease stops us in our tracks, it is too late to realize that stress was the culprit that opened the door.

Stress is not a silent killer. It is shouting at us from every corner! To mismanage stress is to mismanage our chance at life. It is estimated that 70 percent of all physician office visits are for stress-related illnesses. Workers in the United States consume fifteen tons of aspirin every day. Soon job stress will be the number one reason for workman's compensation.[1] Yet, as strange as it may seem, stress is NOT our enemy. It is the mismanagement of stress that creates trouble, not the existence of stress itself. Properly utilized, stress is one of our greatest allies.

## ADRENALIN: GOD'S GO-JUICE

When Hans Selye discovered what he would later call "stress," he was slightly off course from his original intent. He had set out to study the impact of sex hormones, but as he continued to chase the complicated chain of human chemical reactions, he found the key players he really needed to investigate were the hormones of the adrenal gland.[2] As far as stress was concerned, this was the place where the action was. It was here that he found a direct measurement that could be coordinated with bodily damage. Adrenalin in the proper amounts used for a short period of time helped the body. Too much adrenalin over too long a time destroyed.

Adrenalin has many impacts on the body. It increases heart rate and blood pressure. Stomach acid and digestion also speed up under the influence of adrenalin. The brain benefits from increased blood flow. Muscles are more tense and breathing is more rapid and deeper, thus increasing the oxygen supply for all parts of the body. I like to think of adrenalin as God's go-juice. It is like a high-octane fuel that revs up the body and gets it ready for action.

When any kind of stressor comes at us, adrenalin is released to help us adapt to challenge. The stressor might be a deadline for work, it could be a family reunion, or it could be dealing with a car that ran a red light. The more we are alarmed by the stressor, the more adrenalin we will recruit to deal with the situation. We need small amounts of this extra push several times each day. It is good for us. It can even aid our bodies in healing. Remember Selye's experiments with rats? When the irritant placed in the pocket on their backs was mild, the group placed under stress healed faster than their resting counterparts!

Obviously, if a certain amount of stress-produced adrenalin can cure and energize us, and too much can kill us, it would be beneficial to understand how much is too much. If we had some early warning system that could tell us when we were getting near the edge, perhaps we could stop ourselves before going over the cliff! The good news is that there are such measurements, and we can learn to read the early warning signals that our body is sending.

Remember the stress triad from the last chapter? Adrenalin always impacts the (1) stomach, (2) adrenal glands, and (3) thymus/lymph nodes. We may not be able to pull out a lymph node in order to examine our immune system or hold our adrenal gland in our hand to look for swelling. We may not be able to determine how much and what kinds of acid our stomach is churning out. But we can look at a few secondary symptoms that tell us if these organs are getting in trouble. By considering these secondary symptoms, we can get a rough idea if we are using our go-juice in effective ways or destructive ones.

As you read through the four stages of adrenalin recruitment, be brutally honest and ask yourself, "How close to the edge am I living?"

## FOUR STAGES OF ADRENALIN RECRUITMENT

It is fairly easy to identify the level at which our body is using adrenalin. You don't need a lab test and you don't have to prick yourself with a needle. All you have to do is be sensitive and listen to what the body is "saying." Most texts on the subject divide it into four stages. The first stage is when adrenalin is being used as it should. We could say the lights are green and all systems are "go." The next three levels are stages of stress that need our attention. They are like traffic lights that change from yellow to red to *crash!*

### Stage One: Green Light

The first stage of adrenalin recruitment needs no special consideration. This stage is the rise and fall of adrenalin in the blood all during the day that is good for us. It corresponds to the demands of daily living and helps us over the humps of life. We need more go-juice when performing quick or complex mental tasks or when rapid physical responses are called for. We need less adrenalin when life returns to a steady lope. Ideally, we will cycle away from our need of adrenalin and into resting states several times every day. This is how adrenalin was designed to work. This is healing and safety.

The primary element for the success of this stage is that our bodies are coming back down to a complete rest *several times* during the day. This kind of rest does not necessarily mean inactivity, although that element may be involved. More than anything else, these are brief spaces of time when we feel no pressure. We are not running in high gear. One could say that we internally and externally feel at peace.

For example, if we were following a young, stay-at-home mother and had some way of magically measuring her blood-adrenal levels, we might find the following:

When this young woman first wakes up, her adrenalin would be very low, but it would immediately begin to rise as the baby starts crying and the pressure of getting everyone off for work and school begins. The level would fall as the rush of the morning passes and routine chores are begun.

By noon, everything is in high gear again while she is shopping and feeling pressure to get back home. Mid-afternoon, another rest occurs as she puts the baby down for a nap and picks up a magazine for a few moments. Evening is another rushed time. There is supper to provide, homework to check, and kids to bathe. Late evening, there is another dip for a short while before bed. Sex would bring a sharp rise, and sleep the lowest levels of adrenalin that are experienced during our twenty-four-hour monitoring period.

While this example may seem almost artificially obvious, if adrenalin recruitment is being used as it should, a similar pattern would be present whether this woman were a teacher, politician, or plastic surgeon. All occupations must have times of rest that intersperse times of high demand.

Consider yesterday. Did you repeatedly come down to a state of rest? Were you going strong from morning to night? Perhaps you found yourself feeling as though you were under pressure even when engaging in outward signs of rest! Remember that rest does not necessarily imply total inactivity. Rather, it is a sense of peace combined with a slowing of activity. If you do not repeatedly experience rest many times during the day, illness is probably beating a steady cadence as it marches your way.

## Stage Two: Yellow Light

In the second stage, our use of adrenalin has begun to drift into the danger zone. We have been hitting our supply too heavily and warning signs are beginning to show. At this stage, there will be specific indicators that flash a warning much like a yellow traffic light.

Like traffic lights, it is easy to rush past these signs and, if we are lucky, no notable damage will be done. At least, there will be no immediate damage. However, if we continue to ignore the warnings, they will become more intense until they eventually lead to a breakdown. It is normal to have some of these signs occasionally, but if you consistently see the signs—especially if they are daily—pay attention!

1. *Irritability.* One of the first signs that adrenalin is getting out of hand is irritability. We get angry at the traffic and yell at the kids, then later wonder why we were such a jerk.

2. *Cold Hands and Feet.* As adrenalin prepares the body to adapt, it pulls the blood away from the extremities and increases circulation in the brain and body trunk. This is an excellent move if you are running from a tiger or desperately trying to figure out a problem, but it is rather useless for twenty-four-hour living.

3. *Feeling Constantly Pressured.* It is perfectly normal to feel pressured when deadlines or other time-sensitive issues must be met. But many of us feel pressured even when there is no deadline. A long line at the store is not the end of the world and probably will not make three minutes' difference in our schedule, but we may feel enormous pressure when we have to wait. Do you tap your foot and tell the microwave to hurry up?

4. *Headaches in the Early Morning and Late Evening.* Adrenalin has a numbing effect. Therefore, when adrenalin

levels are high, we don't notice the headache, but when it falls—as is common in the early morning or late evening—we notice the pain. You have probably heard people say, "I'm all right once I get on with the day." Perhaps you have even said this yourself and assumed that you just needed to "shake it off" or "get busy and forget about it." Because adrenalin can act much like two aspirins, ignoring the pain until it goes away will work . . . until the crash.

Does the above list sound familiar? Don't stop reading yet. Because the *general adaptation syndrome* (stress) is operating at all levels of adrenalin recruitment, the symptoms of each stage will be similar. While some symptoms are unique to certain stages, many of the warning signs differ only in the matter of degree. Your body may be flashing you a yellow light, but read on. That may change.

## Stage Three: Red Light

During stage three, we have become chronic users of our biological high-octane fuel. The blood levels of adrenalin may change from elevated to very elevated during the day, but they will seldom return to the low level of rest. The yellow warning light has now turned red, and symptoms will be harder to ignore.

1. *Chronically Cold Hands and Feet.* This is similar to a yellow-light symptom, but now it is chronic, not occasional.

2. *Headaches, Twenty-Four to Thirty-Six Hours into Rest Cycle.* At this stage, the headaches, which had been mild and daily, have "improved." If there are no times of rest, there may be fewer headaches because the adrenalin levels stay chronically high. However, when rest is attempted on a vacation or perhaps on a weekend, headaches and other pains may return.

3. *Feeling "Antsy."* Another problem that will occur when we try to rest is that we will internally feel very ill at ease. Somehow rest does not "feel good" anymore. Even though the body may obviously be tired, the internal motor is still running full tilt, resulting in emotional discomfort. A common term is that we feel, "antsy."

4. *Sleep Disturbances.* There is a direct correlation between sleep and adrenalin levels. When adrenalin is chronically high, we may have trouble unwinding from sleep. I often hear clients say, "I could get to sleep at night if I could just turn off my brain!" This is an indication that your body's accelerator is stuck on high. You may even have become addicted to your own adrenalin.

4. *Early Morning Lethargy.* Because adrenalin falls during the night, you may find morning extremely difficult. Two cups of coffee, a little worry over the coming events of the day, and a cold shower may bring the adrenalin levels back up to their chronic level. When it does, you may feel better, but this is a temporary solution and will not last.

### Stage Four: CRASH

By the time a person reaches stage four, the analogy of traffic lights is no longer applicable. This is a crash. In previous stages, we could ignore or push past the problems. Now, that becomes impossible. No matter how much we push, things only become worse. Neither exercise nor sleep will truly relax the body or the mind. Any relief that these activities bring will be short lived, if they occur at all. This is sometimes called "hitting the wall" or "burnout." It will not go away, and it cannot be cured by a couple of days off.

At this stage, the adrenal glands are swollen and in real trouble. Their production of hormones has become confused and will be disconnected from bodily demands. Adrenalin may suddenly shoot very high for no apparent reason (panic attack), or it may not be there at all (apathy) when we have a task that would normally require us to swing into high gear.

1. *Depression.* This is one of the first symptoms indicating burnout. A large number of people who come to my office are depressed because of exhaustion rather than for classical reasons, such as repressed anger, childhood issues, or brain chemical disorders. As a nation, we are worn out.

2. *Frequent Illnesses.* Because the thymus and lymph nodes are major players in the defense system, anything that impacts

their function also impacts our ability to fight such things as colds, stomach flu, etc. Excessive adrenalin recruitment will lower our immune system to the point that we will catch everything that comes along.

3. *Chronic Fatigue.* By this stage, there will be no doubt that you are tired. Unbelievable, bone-deep, can't-shake-it, just-shot-me tired. Even if a bit of rest or an unexpected adrenalin surge blesses you with a day or two of revival, it will evaporate like a mist, and the weariness will return.

4. *Anxiety and/or Panic Attacks.* Because adrenalin production has been divorced from actual need, your body may dump a load of chemicals into the blood stream at the most unexpected moments. I have never had a panic attack, but when clients describe them to me they often say they felt as though they were going to die. Specific symptoms are unique to each individual, but most say that their heart races, chest hurts, hands shake, sweat breaks out, and limbs become weak. But the worst part is the feeling of utter, impending doom that consumes them.

5. *Apathy.* Like depression, apathy often accompanies burnout. There is just no energy to care about anything anymore. The apathy is often so deep that it is like moving through a fog. Familiar things become foreign. Life and people have a sense of artificiality. Everything is surreal.

Considering the consequences of moving from stage two to stage four, it is of utmost importance that we learn to listen to our bodies. We may speed past the warning light or even the red light, but when true burnout occurs, the recovery time—with good care—will be ***one to three years!***

## MEASURING YOUR BODY STRESS

Our body is more than a convenient tool. It is a vital part of being human. God thought so much of the body that he provided for a resurrection, thus indicating that a soul is incomplete without a body. The body is marvelously designed with many early warning systems, but for many of us, ignoring the body's alarm bells has become a way of life or even a boasting.

Complaining to a boss, coworker or mate that we are "burned out" can be another way of saying, "Don't bother me right now. I am important and the world can't run without me." This seems especially true in the ministry. It is time we slowed down and listened to what our bodies are trying to tell us.

To aid you in listening to your body and judging how close you may be to the physical edge, take a moment to fill in the following test. This was taken from Dr. Archibald Hart's excellent work *The Hidden Link Between Adrenalin and Stress.*[3] It is used here with his permission.

For each of the twenty items that follow, you should give a numerical answer ranging from 0 to 3. In each blank, you should list a number according to how often that particular item is true. When you finish, add your score.

## Physical Symptoms of Excessive Stress
### Score Key:
0= I do not experience this symptom at all.

1= I sometimes experience this symptom (perhaps once a month).

2= I frequently experience this symptom (more than once a month, but not more than once a week).

3= I often experience this symptom (once a week or more).

### Test:
_____1. Do you experience headaches of any sort?

_____2. Do you experience tension or stiffness in your neck, shoulders, jaw, arms, or stomach?

_____3. Do you have nervous ticks, or do you tremble?

_____4. Do you feel your heart thumping or racing?

_____5. Do you get irregular heartbeats, or does your heart skip beats?

_____6. Do you have difficulty breathing at times?

_____7. Do you ever get dizzy or lightheaded?

_____8. Do you feel as though you have a lump in your throat or have to clear it?

_____9.   Do you suffer from colds, the flu, or hoarseness?

_____10. Are you bothered by indigestion, nausea, or discomfort in your stomach?

_____11. Do you have diarrhea or constipation?

_____12. Do you bite your nails?

_____13. Do you have difficulty falling or staying asleep?

_____14. Do you wake up feeling tired?

_____15. Are your hands or feet cold?

_____16. Do you grind or grit your teeth, or do your jaws ache?

_____17. Are you prone to excess perspiration?

_____18. Are you angry or irritable?

_____19. Do you feel a lot of generalized pain?

_____20. Have you become aware of increased anxiety, worry, fidgetiness, or restlessness?

_____ Total Score

If you have a total score of less than ten, you may need to go back and take the test again. You may also want to check your pulse! Some physical symptoms of stress are normally present. If your score was this low, you are either not being honest with yourself or you have a most unusually relaxed life. If the latter is true, put this book down. Your time could more profitably be used elsewhere!

For a score of eleven to twenty, your stress is probably not creating excessive physical problems at this time. There may be some event that has your stress slightly elevated, but as long as you can balance that stress with times of rest you are probably all right. Whatever you are doing to manage the stress in your life, keep it up. The system is working.

When the score for physical symptoms of stress falls between twenty-one and thirty, stress is beginning to take a physical toll that will likely result in damage to the body. A score in this category may indicate that there are one or two stressing events currently hassling you. You are managing them fairly well, but you should exert great caution.

If a score this high continues, it can do as much damage as a higher score endured for a less lengthy period of time. The body can take only so much stress for so long without physical problems being added to stressors already in your life. This level is a flashing yellow light warning you of danger ahead.

A score between thirty-one and forty is a red light. This is not an anticipation of probable trouble. This means that trouble is already on your doorstep. You may be experiencing life as exciting or it may feel very distressing, but no matter how you feel emotionally, your body is telling you that things are out of control. It is important that you find a way to back off the edge. Either use this stress management program or some other, but *get busy and do something!*

If you have a score of over forty-one, you have raced past the red light and you are headed for a wall. You should strongly consider making an appointment with a counselor or medical practitioner or both.

## MEASURING YOUR MENTAL STRESS

Damaging levels of stress can be brought on by the trials we face, but that is not the only source. It's not just what happens to us, but the way we respond that makes the difference. It is not only external forces, but internal ones that change profitable tension into destructive wear. When it comes to stress, our mental attitude makes all the difference.

When we use an excessive amount of energy to deal with small situations, our resources quickly become depleted. The same thing is true if we fill our lives with multiplied levels of business and race through each day attempting to cover all the bases. People who habitually conduct their lives this way are sometimes called *Type A* personalities. The following test has been designed to help you measure whether or not you are among that group of people. This test was originally published in the work of Dr. Hart and is gratefully used with his permission.

## Type A Personality

### Score Key:
0= does not apply
1=less than once a month
2=more than once a month
### Test:

_____I feel there is not enough time in each day to do all the things I need to do.

_____I tend to speak faster than other people, even finishing their sentences for them.

_____My spouse or friends say that I eat too quickly.

_____I tend to get very upset when I loose a game.

_____I am very competitive in work, sports, or games.

_____I tend to be bossy and dominate others.

_____I prefer to lead rather than to follow.

_____I become impatient when I have to wait.

_____I tend to make decisions quickly or even impulsively.

_____I regularly take on more than I can accomplish.

_____I become irritable (even angry) more often than most people.

_____I feel pressured for time even when I am not doing something that is important.

_____ Total Score

If your total score was zero to five, you definitely are not a *Type A* person. You may slip into the behavior once in a while, but it is not enough to be a problem.

If your score is between six and ten, you show occasional signs of *Type A* behavior. You may have a temporary irritation in your life that will relent, but you are approaching a pervasive *Type A* pattern as you near the upper end of this score.

From eleven to sixteen, you show definite signs of being a *Type A* personality. At the upper end of this score you are showing signs of excessive adrenalin recruitment and are likely to be experiencing signs of distress.

If your score was above seventeen, according to Dr. Hart, you are not only a *Type A* personality, but

> "you are living dangerously. Life may be very miserable for you, or it may be very exciting, but either way you are likely to develop cardio-vascular deterioration if you do not change your lifestyle. If you smoke or have any other risk factors such as diabetes or high blood pressure, or a family history of heart disease, you should seek professional help as soon as possible."

About 50 percent of the U.S. population will grade themselves as *Type A* and about 40 percent of the population will show as *Type B*. It doesn't take much math knowledge to figure out that doesn't add up. There is a third category, but it is rare. Only about 10 percent of the population fall into it. The category is for those individuals who are both strongly A and strongly B. These are people who when they work, they work hard, and when they sit, they sit loose. They have learned how to both gear up and get the job done and also how to come back down to times of real and deep rest. And they alternate between the two poles according to need. As best I can understand from the many tests that I have personally taken, I likely fall in this A/B category, but I don't think I was born that way. Time and much practice has shaped my personality to respond quite differently than I would have several years ago.

Knowing whether we are a *Type A, B,* or *A/B* personality is more than an academic exercise. It can be a wakeup call that saves your life. *Type A* men are three times as likely to experience heart disease as *Type B*. As medical research reports continue to link disease and stress, knowing whether they are studying your type could help you know whether the research applies personally.

However, simply knowing how much stress has damaged us or how we characteristically respond to the mild stressors of life is not enough. Once we know our scores, we need to do something about them. What can we do? That is what the next chapter is all about.

# CHAPTER 3

# Choices:
# The Key to Lower Stress

The answer to stress is simple. We just have to make different choices. But how can we make choices when nothing in our day is optional? Choosing to rest can seem as impossible as choosing to fly!

When I tell counseling clients that the solution to their stress is a willingness to make choices, I am guaranteed a responding look of either confusion or anger. Choices? Of course they would like to choose a slower-paced life! Who wouldn't want a break from the strain that is killing them? He would gladly choose to quit his high-stress job and go on a month's vacation to Hawaii! Or, she would be delighted to choose to let hubby take care of the kids for a few days while she goes to a spa in the mountains.

The problem is that the realities of life make such ideal times of rest impossible. Yet, being intently aware that real choices exist and being actively involved in the process of choosing the one **and only** proven element will keep the pressures of life from destroying our bodies before their natural expiration date.

Before we examine the fifteen stress-busting ideas that I will suggest, we need to examine the dynamics of choice. If you are like most people, you have had too many experiences where good intentions faded into the status quo. You acquired information, thought about change, agreed that change would be good, and, perhaps, even took a few steps toward the goal, but life got in the way. In the end, nothing changed.

## LESSONS FROM A TRAPPED RAT

The concept of choice and its ability to ameliorate the damaging effects of stress was, like many other aspects of stress, demonstrated by Dr. Selye and his rats. All of Dr. Selye's experiments were interesting, but the ones that tested the free will of rats were ingenious.

Dr. Selye took two rats that were identical in health and weight and wired each rat electronically to receive a radio signal that was painful. He placed the rats in identical boxes and fed them both the same food. The rats were alike in every way except one. He taught rat **B** a trick and just let rat **A** go on about his ratty way.

When everything was set, Dr. Selye began his experiment by briefly turning on a signal that delivered pain to each rat through the wires that had been implanted. The pain was the same for each rat. But alone in their box, neither of them knew that another rat was hurting just on the other side of the wall. When rat **B** did his trick, the electronic pain was turned off, thus instantly stopping the pain for both rats. Day after day the pain would come in varying amounts to each rat, but as soon as rat **B** did his trick, the pain would cease.

Rat **B** only had a rat-size brain but even he could figure out that there was a connection between stopping the pain and performing the trick. When pain started, he had a choice. He could do something that would make a difference. For rat **A**, the experience was very different. He received no more pain than rat **B** but he never knew why the pain started or what made it stop. He had no choice.

At the end of the experiment, the rats were put to sleep and their stress triad examined for signs of damage.[1] Sure enough, the rat who had a choice showed little damage, but the rat that experienced no choice was very diseased and dying.

The official definition of stress given by Dr. Selye runs about half a page of fine print, but the shorthand version is that stress is *the life energy that is being expended to enable an organism to adapt to change.* Going from a state of rest to the experience of pain required an adaptation for each rat. Both were stressed! But the rat that experienced a sense of control over what happened developed only minimal damage to his body. The trapped rat died.

## CHOICE AND LOSS

Knowing we have choices, choosing and enjoying the results of those choices is the *only* way to manage stress. But because we are humans, our experience of choice is very different from that of brother rat. When we choose one thing, we automatically lose those things that we did not choose. It is the sense of loss that keeps us trapped as we refuse to deal with this reality.

The story is told of a little boy in a candy store who walked in with a big grin and two shiny new quarters in his hand. He looked at the row of bins containing jelly beans and jaw breakers and lemon drops and chocolate balls. He walked back and forth studying the options and chewing on his fingers.

At first, he chose the jelly beans. But then he realized that if he got jelly beans, he could not have the chocolate. For fifteen minutes he walked back and forth. Each time he choose one thing, he quickly changed his mind, because carrying through with the decision meant he would loose something else. Even to buy a combination of choices meant that he would lose his quarters. In the end, he walked out with a frown.

Unless we deal with the reality that making any choice means that we loose something, we will never be able to implement any stress-reduction program based on choice and options. The hardest thing you will probably have to give up is a secret belief that most of us harbor in a dark corner of our minds: the belief that we can have it all, do it all, control it all, and create more hours in a day! Hopefully, the peace and increased health that you gain will far outweigh any mild sense of loss.

## I THINK I CAN, I THINK I CAN

As children, most of us read the story *The Little Engine That Could*. Little Engine was faced with an impossible hill to climb and an impossible load to pull, but with encouragement from others and by repeatedly reassuring himself with *"I think I can, I think I can,"* the Little Engine made it over the hill and safely brought his cargo to the children on the other side.

That short story of courage and faith is excellent for proper training of hope in the young, but can be a recipe for disaster when translated into adult self-expectations. We too often keep telling ourselves that with a little more effort we can do the impossible. We honestly believe that with a little more credit we can have the unaffordable, or with a few more false smiles everyone will love us, or if we will pull on our own boot straps a little harder no dream will be beyond us. We push ourselves because with a little more effort we can do the task perfectly. We take on impossible loads built of small responsibilities, any one of which would be doable but when added together mount to the sky.

Our problem is that like the frog that was put on to boil, our self-expectations come on us incrementally and we don't know we are in trouble until it is too late. The process goes something like this: We reason that *it* is only a small thing to add to the schedule, and after all, the church needs it, or no one else would do it, or the kids are depending on it, or it would not take much more effort to do it *right*. Then all the little things that would take just a small amount of effort add up and we are trapped.

### I Can't Have It All

The *it* in our discussion refers to things. This is about *stuff*. We all want stuff. We need stuff. There is nothing wrong with having lots of stuff. But have you ever considered how stuff dominates your life? In a very real sense, stuff own us, not vice versa. On one level, we know we can't have it all. But down deep, like the Little Engine, we hang on to the illogical assumption that we really CAN have everything we want if we try hard enough.

33

And, when we try to let go of stuff, our souls are loath to decide which part we must do without! It is one thing to know that we will never possess everything. But when the abstract becomes practical and the part we don't possess is just beyond our grasp, the situation somehow changes.

I received a call the other day from a frantic wife. She wanted to see a counselor that very day because her husband had impulsively bought a dog. She was panicked with thoughts of feeding, care, boarding, veterinary bills, and the kids' crying in future years as the dog grew old and died. While not necessarily agreeing with her overreaction, most of us can understand the burden of responsibility and limitation of personal freedom connected with the purchase of a dog. But can we as easily see that *every* object we take into our possession binds us? It does not have to be alive in order to make demands of us.

Every object we own took energy to select. It took energy to earn the money to buy. It still takes energy as we use, store, clean, insure, and move it. We stay home to wait for someone to repair it. We spend hours in research because we need an upgrade/new/larger version of it. All this has the illusion of importance, but the truth is that the thing holding us captive and sapping our strength is an inanimate object that cares nothing for us and will likely end up in someone's garage sale!

In our materialistic society, stuff has crept in creating a silent tyranny over our lives. The tyranny is not all bad because we humans need objects. Beds and hair dryers and cars and computers are all important stuff. It would be impossible to live in modern America without them but there is a down side we dare not forget. Things not only give to us, they also take from us. They take a small slice of what Selye called *life adaptation energy.*

Figuring out how much of our limited life energy we are willing to give to objects is a part of stress management. This is not as simple a job as it may appear to be. It means we will have to do without something we could obtain if we stretched for it. We will have to say no. Having more life may mean that we choose to have less stuff.

## I Can't Do It All

Another limitation is the obvious reality that we can't be in two places at once. Even Little Engine could not do that. But like the knowledge that we can't have it all, this reality is often known by the brain and ignored by the soul.

I am continually amazed when clients step to the appointment desk and I overhear them trying to set their next visit with my secretary.

"What about a day appointment?"

"Sorry, I work during the day."

"Can you come next Thursday evening at seven?"

"No, there is basketball practice that night."

"Can I schedule you for Monday?"

"I'll be taking a course at the community college that night. Does she work Saturday afternoon?"

It can take longer to set next week's appointment than it did to do the counseling! People often put so much on their schedules that the only way they could meet the demands is to instantly clone themselves.

The logical brain knows that while we are attending our eight-year-old's soccer game, we cannot also be across town checking on a real-estate deal and at the same time attending a pottery class. But how many of us have demonstrated that we think we can if we will just exert enough effort and cut enough corners?

We race away from the soccer game twenty minutes early, apologizing for not seeing the ending and asking a neighbor to take our son home while we check with the real-estate agent by car phone and show up late for the pottery class for which we paid dearly (after all, we needed to have *something* for ourselves in the schedule)! The result is that we are never really present no matter where we are because the next place we need to be is occupying 50 percent of our mind!

## I Can't Control It All

Another thing that we know logically, but somehow never manage to deal with on a practical level, is the fact that complete control is an illusion. We are not, and have never been, in complete control of anything, but we pressure ourselves into acting and feeling as though we are responsible for just such an impossible feat. We can not control circumstances, other people, or even our own emotions. We influence these things and decide how we will respond to them, but we don't control them.

If we would strike off our *to-do* list all those things over which we have no direct power and concentrate only on using our influence as best we know, our stress level would go down considerably.

The family I saw last week was typical of the tangled knots that sometime snare even the best-intentioned individuals. Dad had left the family several years before, leaving a mom and three teens. The home was in chaos. Everyone tried to talk at once. Everyone was excusing his or her own actions and telling all the other family members what they should do. Everyone went home tense that night, including the counselor!

One of the most consistent goals I have to accomplish with clients such as that is to help them understand the difference between what they need to control and what they need to release. To accomplish that goal, I often use some kind of visual. One such illustration is based on the letter of St. Paul to the Ephesians.

Ephesians 6:10-17 is familiar to most Christians. This is the passage where the apostle Paul urges the followers of Christ to fight against evil. He uses the analogy of the armor of a Roman soldier and urges us to "Put on the whole armor of God." He spends much time drawing lessons from the soldier's helmet, belt, shield, and sword. Many sermons have been preached on each of these concepts, but another portion of this analogy is not so well known, even though it is mentioned repeatedly in the verses. Paul tells us to "take your stand"; "be able to stand your ground," and "stand firm." He also refers to "having done all to stand" (NIV). Twice the concept of *stand* is personalized. It is *YOUR* stand and *YOUR* ground. This would have meant a lot to a Roman soldier because in addition to his personal helmet he also had a personal stand.

Before Rome, the primary battle formation was a tight knot of eight men. They stood so close to one another that their shields overlapped. The theory was that this tight knot would be impervious to the enemy. Rome changed all that and spread their men in an open line with space between each soldier. As the battles took place, each soldier was trained to concentrate on the small space for which he was personally responsible. Only limited attention was to be given to anything going on outside this personal stand. His sole job was to take orders, defend that small territory to the death, and leave the big picture to others. Giving each soldier a space or *stand* was a new concept, and with that concept Rome conquered the world.

Occasionally, I will have clients draw a stick figure representing a Roman soldier and then to place a circle around him to represent his stand. I ask them to place things in their lives either inside or outside the circle according to whether or not it falls within the realm of their control.

Their mother's disapproval of their high credit-card debt? Outside. Their resentment against their mother? Inside. The existence of their three-year-old's temper tantrum? Outside. Their reaction to their three-year-old's tantrum? Inside. Losing twenty pounds of excess weight? Outside. Whether or not they eat the cookie that is in their hand? Inside.

Visualizing this simple picture can help us get a reality check when our souls take on things for which our logic knows we are not responsible. It is very much akin to the Serenity Prayer: *"God grant me the serenity to accept the things I can not change / The courage to change the things I can / And the wisdom to know the difference."*

Life is filled with unexpected turns and twists. No matter how hard we try to get it all together, life in the real world will keep scrambling our planned schedules and reprioritizing our carefully made list. Last week I heard someone say that if you want to hear God laugh, just tell Him about your plans for tomorrow! It is imperative that we hold our plans and desire for control in very open hands.

## I Can't Create More Time

It is obvious that unless a person is being born or is dying, we all have the same amount of time in each day. Time is controlled by the universe, not by our will and effort. Yet, even though our logical minds understand that fact, our behavior suggests that deep down we believe the limitations of time don't apply to us personally. Limitations are for the rest of humanity.

I used to think that I must have been born a week late and never managed to catch up. Each day seemed to be just about four hours shorter than it needed to be. In those days, I was a young mother, and the demands never seemed to let up. The more I tried to do, the more remained to be done. Finally, I decided to make up the difference by treating sleep as though it were an optional luxury.

My husband worked shift work at the time and I was often alone at night, so I hit upon the idea of using the night hours for waxing floors, or study, or sewing—all the tasks that were hard to do with children hanging on my skirt. Once I became accustomed to the late hours, I wasn't even bothered by drowsiness, and getting up in the morning was no harder than it had always been.

I thought my scheme was working out quite well when my plans were interrupted by illness. At least, I thought it was illness. My strength began to melt away. The broom gained weight and the back steps grew as tall as a mountain. I began to misjudge distances and knock over glasses instead of picking them up. I was dull witted and kept bumping into doors. Tired blood? I wondered.

Finally, I went to our family doctor. I was sure I had something awful. After I gave him a list of symptoms, he asked, "What time do you go to bed?"

I eyed him curiously. "Between one and two. Why?"

"And what time do you get up?"

"Five forty-five. Why?"

"How many times do you get up with the children during the night?"

"I'd guess an average of three times. Why?"

38

"There is nothing wrong with you that is not wrong with 98 percent of the young mothers who come through this clinic. You are sleepy."

I thought my dear physician had finally popped his cork. Sleepy? What kind of diagnosis was that? I didn't feel sleepy.

"If you will slow down, unwind, and get some sleep, all your symptoms will disappear," he told me.

I didn't believe a word he said, but the next day I ran into a door and bruised my face, so I decided to give more sleep a try. To my amazement, within a week most of the symptoms had vanished.

God has trapped mankind inside strict, twenty-four-hour time brackets. And He has ordained necessities within those brackets that cannot be avoided. It takes time to eat, time to sleep, time to form relationships, time for personal care, and even time for sex! Fully half of the couples that come to my office with concerns over their sex life in truth have a time problem, not a biological malfunction. If they would sell the television, stop working overtime, and take time to visit with each other over a light beverage for half an hour before bed, most of their sex problems would disappear.

Time restrictions were set by the Maker of the universe, and altering that setup is not part of our job description. We may do a better or worse job of managing our time, but the reality of its limits is bigger than we are. The sooner we yield to that reality the less stressed we will be.

## I THINK I'LL CHOOSE

Helping you to understand the choices that are available to help reduce stress and encouraging you to make those choices is what this book is all about. However, your first choice is to recognize the limitations of life in the real world. We can't have it all, do it all, control it all, or change the number of hours in a day. What we can do is learn to choose wisely where we will spend our energy and to make the choice of yielding to reality when the way we would prefer is blocked.

The rats in Dr. Selye's experiment had no choice about whether or not they experienced pain. The reality of pain was beyond their control. But when the perception of choice was added to the equation, pain lost much of its ability to damage. We are not rats in a cosmic maze but we can feel like that when unmovable realities block our way. It is important that we exercise the choices that are available to us, but it is *vitally* important that we recognize we have choices—even when the only choice we can make is to yield ourselves in faith to a difficult situation.

In the next four chapters you will be presented with fifteen possible choices. Five choices will require no time investment at all. Three choices will require one to fifteen minutes and three others will require thirty minutes to two hours. I will suggest three options that require twenty-four to seventy-two hours. The last suggestion is one of attitude, which is a choice you can make even when no choices exist.

Of course, trying to implement fifteen choices this week would add to your stress, not reduce it. NO ONE SHOULD ATTEMPT DRASTIC, SUDDEN CHANGES. Remember, the goal is to *reduce* stress, not to add more items to an already overcrowded agenda. It would be far better to choose one no-time-required item and do it well than to attempt drastic changes and beat yourself up for being a "failure."

For most people, a good program would be to read through the next five chapters, then go to the appendix and pick one or two ideas that seem workable. Make a commitment to practice the technique(s) for one week. At the end of the first week, reevaluate. You can either continue with your previous choices or select a different stress-reducing idea from the list. Practice for one more week and reevaluate once again.

Repeat the procedure for a third week for a total of 21 days. For many people, twenty-one days is enough time to establish a habit. Replacing the habit of stress with a habit of rest is your goal. Enjoying the freedom of choices well made and expectations that are held in very open hands will be your peace.

CHAPTER 4

# Stress Busters:
# No Time Required

**#1—How Much Am I Paying?**
**#2—Putting on the Brakes**
**#3—Practice Body Awareness**
**#4—Coming in for a Landing**
**#5—Musical Notes**

Most people agree that they need to reduce their stress. Hopefully, for those reading this book, this is more than just a theoretical agreement. I trust you have taken the test in the previous chapters and are *convinced* that the situation is serious and you that need to take concrete steps.

Now, the problem is what steps to take and how painful will it be? Wanting to reduce the pressure is one thing. How to do it is an entirely different matter. The calendar on the kitchen wall fills up with appointments for ball games, rehearsals, and shifting carpool assignments. Our job demands increase and the boss is considering moving the entire operation to another state. Logic tells us that everything can't be priority one, but nothing on our to-do list volunteers for second place! We want to slow down and find a way to relax our body and our mind, but how?

At times like these, it is good to know that some techniques for stress management do not require a single moment of time commitment. You don't have to add a thing to your "to-do" list. You don't have to purchase special equipment, travel anywhere, or exert a lot of self discipline, or even stop what you are doing. These stress busters take place entirely in the mind, and you don't even have to use 100 percent of that! Unless you are actively engaged in brain surgery or some other all-consuming task, you can practice any of these techniques with minimum effort and without breaking stride from normal activities.

In this chapter you will find five different techniques for reducing stress that require no time. Zero. Zilch. When you plan your twenty-one-day program and choose your stress-relief tactics, I would strongly suggest that at least one of the stress busters come from this list. Stress is, more than anything else, a mental activity. Using mental counter measures just makes good sense.

## STRESS BUSTER #1: HOW MUCH AM I PAYING?

One very easy stress buster is to simply get in a habit of asking yourself how much you are "paying" in stress and what are you "buying" with that expenditure. You may find that you are often spending much and getting almost nothing in return.

For instance, if you are in a grocery line and the person in front of you suddenly decides to exchange three items, how much emotional energy do you expend as you adapt to that situation? Do you tap your foot, getting more angry by the moment? Look repeatedly at your watch? Is your mind whirling while you think about where you have to be next?

The next time you are in a situation such as this, ask yourself, "What am I *buying* with all this energy I am giving out?" Often you are *buying* nothing at all. Even if you could use your energy to make the clerk move faster or the customer get out of the way, what have you gained? One minute? Two? How much will you have paid for that brief amount of time? Was the stress expenditure really worth it?

This becomes vitally important when we realize that our adaptation resources are as limited as any other resource. Stress, by definition, is *the amount of life energy that we give out while adapting to change.* That life energy is finite.

Few of us recognize the reality of our finite resources. One reason for this is our daily experience. We cycle repeatedly through waking and sleep, activity and rest. We continually expend and are refreshed. This can fool us into believing that the amount of energy we expend can be replaced. And while it is true that refreshment occurs, the amount of refreshment we gain is never quite equal to the energy that was expended. The tiny energy deficit that we are building is imperceptible until it catches us unaware.

> Many people believe that after they have exposed themselves to various stressful activities a rest can restore them to where they were before. This is false. Experiments on animals have clearly shown that each exposure leaves an indelible scar in that it uses reserves of adaptability which can not be replaced. It is true that immediately after some harassing experience, rest can restore us to almost the original level of fitness by eliminating acute fatigue. But the emphasis is on the word *almost.* Since we constantly go through periods of stress and rest during life, even a minute deficit of adaptation energy every day slowly adds up. It adds up to what we call aging.
>
> Hans Selye, *Stress of Life*

One way to think of this concept is to imagine that each of us has been born with a specific amount of life energy in some bank of the eternal. Every night as we sleep we draw a certain amount of energy out of that bank and put it in our "wallet" where it can be used. All during the day we are spending the resources in that wallet.

A little energy here, a little adaptation there, a little stress over yonder, and slowly the energy in the wallet is depleted. Another night's rest and it is restored. But the total amount available in our internal bank is finite. One day the resources in our "bank" may be so low that our bodies will break under the strain of the deficit.

We can help control the outflow of our dwindling energy supply by careful budgeting. One of the best ways to do this "budgeting" is to put some scale in our mind that helps us measure what we are giving out and what we are getting back for that expenditure. This simple method not only works for stress, but it can work for other situations as well.

I remember one couple who came to me for marriage counseling. After listening to their arguments and struggles, I suggested that they consider how much they were "paying" in energy and stress for each argument between them.? How much did they actually gain by such expenditures? I suggested they put the concept in financial terms. Was this issue they were fighting over worth five cents, or was it worth one dollar of energy? A five-cent issue should only be given five cents' worth of life energy.

There are those rare times when it is almost fun to be a counselor. The very next week the couple came back with much of their tension resolved. They had each committed to think how much the issue was worth before speaking and to "spend" no more than reasonable. They had even learned to "price" the issue when communicating with each other and agreed on a top dollar that any issue could be awarded. If a mate said, "This is a five-dollar issue," the other knew to give it full attention!

If you would like to try this stress-busting technique, resolve to ask yourself many times during the day, *"Is the energy I am spending worth what I am buying?"* If it is not, mentally pull back and refuse to waste your life on things that don't matter. It is a sobering thought to know that when your "bank account" of life adaptation energy is empty, it is empty for good.

## STRESS BUSTER #2: PUTTING ON THE BRAKES

Another proven, no-time stress buster is to simply slow down physical actions. People under stress internally push the clock. They eat, drive, move, and speak at a rapid pace. In reality, these fast actions save very little time and the limited gains that may be made are quickly wiped out by mistakes, high tension, and even illness. Slowing down the actions of the body can slow down and rest the internal world of the soul.

Pushing the clock and excessive time awareness are part of the Type A personality profile. It is also a snowballing dynamic that increases the likelihood that we will be more stressed and pressured. Asking whether we are pressured because we are Type A or whether we must be Type A in order to survive the pressure we are under can be like asking which came first—the chicken or the egg.

Are we irritated because we are late, or are we late because our habitual irritation takes brain energy and therefore we lost the car keys! We race against the clock and it increases our tension. Then the tension brings on a headache and that makes us angry, which in turn makes us race against the clock!

The good news is that we don't always have to figure out which came first before we can address the problem. Like a ring, the cycle of time pressure plus Type A plus tension plus more time pressure can be broken at any point. Often the simplest and most successful way to break the cycle is to slow down common body movements. Making a one-week commitment to slow down just one physical activity will likely spill over into other areas of life.

Have you noticed that you are always the first one finished at the table? For one week, resolve that you will finish last and put down your fork between bites. Do you often interrupt others or talk over them? Resolve that for one week you will talk more slowly and wait before you speak.

A friend of mine once remarked, 'Why do you run everywhere you go? I don't think I have ever seen you *walk* from your car into the store."

The comment surprised me. I was not aware that I rushed from one point to the next, but I took my friend seriously and began to consciously slow my walk. The first day I tried it I was shocked. I got places as quickly as ever, but I was much more relaxed when I arrived. I could literally feel the difference in muscle tension. When I committed myself to step more slowly through the day, the day became easier to cope with because there were fewer tension headaches.

The power of slower body actions to create a slower, calmer internal world can be truly surprising. I once knew a pastor who had a habitual anger problem. He was always losing his temper and then apologizing for it. He was frustrated because God would not fix his anger problem, but at the same time he was resistant to a gentle, internal conviction about his many speeding tickets.

The pastor made no connection between his fast driving and his anger until the conviction became too much and he made the commitment to drive one mile an hour under the speed limit. Within a month, not only had his stress level gone down tremendously, but his anger problem was broken for good.

## STRESS BUSTER #3: PRACTICE BODY AWARENESS

Another no-time-required stress buster is to listen to our body. The body God has given us is an excellent barometer of stress. Unfortunately, we seldom listen to its gentle nudging. The only time we notice it is when it screams for attention or it cannot serve us the way it once did.

Practicing an awareness of the more subtle signals from our body and purposefully responding with muscle relaxation can head off many stress-related problems before they become major concerns. This awareness is not difficult. You don't need special equipment, and there is no need to stop normal activities in order to practice.

Right now, as you read these sentences, you can practice a moment of body awareness. Begin with your face and jaw. Are the muscles tight? Move your jaw gently from side to side and by an act of your will release any tension. Let your thoughts move on to your shoulders and neck. Again, with an act of will, relax the muscles as much as possible. Move your thoughts to your stomach and chest. Take a deep breath and relax those areas. Think of your spine and hip area and consciously release any tension found there. Last of all, notice the muscles in your legs and feet. If you are holding them tight, choose to release them and let them rest.

Often people find that they are habitually holding specific muscles in a tightened position and that mild pain is beginning to develop. Because we are only vaguely aware of the subtle signals, it is easy to race on and ignore the mild discomfort. Only when the discomfort becomes major do we pay attention, and often even then we grab an aspirin or a fifth cup of coffee, thus finding chemical ways to cope rather than learning to relax.

A full-body check of all muscle groups takes less than thirty seconds. Because it is not exercise and involves little or no movement, a body check and muscle relaxation can be done anywhere at any time without disrupting normal activity. Yet, the benefits of this brief act may be large. It may reduce anger, avoid a headache, or preempt an attack of stomach ulcers. The only "difficult" thing is to remember to perform the check!

If you decide to give this stress buster a try, consider setting your watch or beeper to go off three to five times during the day to remind you. No beeper? Concerned that a loud "beep" will catch you at an embarrassing moment? Then why not connect your moment of body awareness with a daily event? Remember to do a body check each time you start your car or before every meal. You will probably need some kind of "trigger" to remind you to check your body for stress signals, but with a little thought you should be able to find a signal that will work for your particular lifestyle.

A second step in body awareness is to be aware of how the foods we eat affect us. Our diets are strongly related to mood, physical stamina, and, most of all, *stress.* However, we often make no conscious connection between the sugared doughnuts we consumed for breakfast and the lethargy and mental fog we experienced mid-morning. I am convinced that if we invested a little mental awareness in making a connection between our food and our physical/mental well being, we might not be such absentminded eaters.

The Standard American Diet is sometimes identified by the achronym S.A.D. One reason for this is that we currently con-sume 159 pounds of sugar per person per year. But sugar is not the only problem. Most of us realize that we eat too much, we eat too fast, and we eat things that damage our bodies. Yet, changing all that would require a major life adjustment, and who has time for *that* project? The good news is that a drastic change is not necessary to reap real benefits. A simple, no-time-required, mental check can encourage us to eliminate a few major offenders.

In my late twenties I had an experience that demonstrated this reality at a practical level. I had not yet put the concept in terms of using body awareness to reduce stress, but the dynamics were the same. Because I didn't drink coffee at that time, it never occurred to me that a sleep problem stressing me out was related to caffeine. Somehow, I did not connect those big, late-night jugs of ice tea with my sleeplessness, until one day the light dawned. Two quarts of iced tea contain much more caffeine that a strong cup of coffee!

Making a change to reduce my stress was not difficult. My Southern heart did not have to give up its beloved tea. No major life changes were required. Listening to my body and changing to decaffeinated after 6 P.M. solved the problem with little pain, no time commitment, and no new items on my to-do list.

Caution: Don't confuse this stress technique with weight loss or cholesterol control or allergies management. Weight-loss diets and other lifestyle changes can reap real benefits, but these are *major* projects that take time and add stress each day. The goal of this program is not to *add* stress to your life, but to *reduce* it.

For stress management, body awareness should be a simple, limited moment that occurs several times during the day when you take a moment to notice any digestive or stomach discomfort and check your energy level. If you notice a problem, think back about what you ate and/or drank during the past two hours. You may need to connect this stress buster with your watch beeper or an event, but it should not add to your daily stress load.

## STRESS BUSTER #4: COMING IN FOR A LANDING

If you were in my office with a stress or anxiety problem, one thing I would likely go over would be an exercise in grounding.

When a person *grounds*, they become intensely aware of their immediate surroundings. They emotionally and physically connected with the present moment. You can ground on any part of the body that touches the outside world. Most often, you need not stop ordinary activities in order to ground. You can even perform a grounding exercise while simultaneously reading this chapter.

When you ground, your attention is drawn to the physical sensations of texture, scent, color, temperature, and weight. As you continue to read, notice how the pages of this book feel in your hands. Let your mind be fully aware of the book's weight and edges.

If you are seated or lying down, take a moment to become fully aware of how it feels for the weight of your body to be held up by the furniture. Think about the temperature of the air on your skin. Simply stated, grounding is the art of being fully present where you are. *All worry is living in the future. All regret is living in the past. Grounding is being present in the now.*

Grounding takes no time from a busy day, but it can add the benefit of less stress. I recall one client who had a lot of trouble driving in Dallas traffic. She would panic and feel as though she had to pull off the road. She avoided certain places at certain times of day and arranged her schedule around traffic conditions.

I taught Susie about grounding, and we practiced several times in the office.[1] First, she grounded on her hands, feeling the texture of the sofa on which she sat. Then we grounded on her feet, putting her full attention on the solidness of the floor and the feeling of her shoes on her feet.

Next, I asked her to close her eyes and imagine herself caught in traffic. She could feel the stress and anxiety rise and her breathing increased and her heart beat faster. While still thinking of the traffic, I asked her to ground on her feet and then her hands.

When she came back the next week, she was ecstatic, "When I began to ground in the present and concentrate on the immediate sensations of my body, I began to feel much more calm," she exclaimed. "I even drove on Central Expressway!"

Grounding is a primary behavior-modification technique for almost any program that addresses anxiety issues. It is simple, easy, and safe. It takes no time out of your day and adds nothing to your schedule. But when you get a message that the boss wants to see you in her office, taking one minute to ground and deeply breathe before you knock on her door can make all the difference in the level of stress you feel.

## STRESS BUSTER #5: MUSICAL NOTES

One of the happiest stress busters that requires no time is to simply sing. Music is one of the few activities that is processed simultaneously in separate major areas of the brain. We occasionally observe this in people who have had strokes that resulted in brain damage. Sometimes these individuals will not be able to speak a word, but they can sing without a problem! It is suspected that this is because the mathematical rhythm of the music activated in one side of the brain opens a neural pathway to the words that are stored in a different place.

When you have a bad day at the office and tensions are high, turn off the radio and throw back your head and sing! Singing is something you can do that requires none of your time, but it can make a large difference in your stress level. The deep breathing and increased oxygen will do your body good and, of course, if you are singing songs with a spiritual or happy message, you get a double bonus. Who knows? You might even find yourself singing as you sail into the future with a more gentle wind at your back.

# CHAPTER 5

# Stress Busters:
# One to Fifteen Minutes

**#6—Meditation**
**#7—A Golden Silence**
**#8—Practice Gratitude**


Shannon rested her head on the back of my office sofa and covered her face with her hands.

"I could go to sleep if there were some way to turn off my brain!" she moaned. "When I am ready to sleep, my brain is as active as that pink bunny in the TV advertisement. It just keeps going and going!"

I inwardly chuckled at Shannon's analogy, but I also sympathized. Not only had I heard this same complaint from other patients, I had experienced it plenty of times myself! It was a great personal relief when I discovered that the pink bunny can be unplugged!

Learning to 'unplug" an overactive brain is a very necessary part of stress relief for most people. How can we enter a state of full rest when thoughts are popping like firecrackers and problems are cycling like a merry-go-round? It can feel like our brain and emotions are stuck on automatic pilot and we can't regain control.

Certain brain malfunctions can make it impossible to 'turn off' unwanted thoughts. For help with these kinds of problems you need a psychiatrist and a prescription pad. But before you rush out to the pharmacy, why not try one of these three basic stress busters that may provide relief without the pills? *Meditation, Progressive Relaxation, and Systematic Gratitude* are easy and non-invasive. And, best of all, the only cost will be a few minutes of your time.

## STRESS BUSTER #6: MEDITATION

There can be many reasons why the body wants to sleep but the brain refuses to rest. Sometimes medications are required or physical problems may be present. But by far the most common reason is—to put it in simple terms—the mind has developed a bad habit. When the billions of tiny electrical connections within the brain, called synapses, have been called upon hour after hour to run at high speed, they more or less get stuck on automatic. Unsticking them is best achieved through the simple, age-old art of meditation.

Meditation has been practiced by contemplative figures in both Eastern and Western cultures. It is an accepted discipline of many religions, including Christianity. The Bible tells us to meditate on three different things. We are to meditate on God (Psalm 63:6) and to meditate on the works of God (Psalm 77:12; 143:5). We are also told to meditate on the word of God (Joshua 1:8; Psalm 119:15).

There are many styles of meditation but most all of them center on some form of mental repetition. It is this slow, repetitive thinking pattern that encourages a slower firing of the brain synapses and provides a sense of internal calm. Through meditation, we literally train our brain to function at a different speed and, like any other training, this may take a little practice. The mind is a very busy place. If you are not accustomed to meditation, your thoughts may be jumping up like popcorn. But in time, the firing of the brain synapses should begin to slow, and you will find yourself able to concentrate on the inward sound of your own silent voice.

### Meditating on the Word

Meditating on a Bible verse is different from just reading it. Of course, you do not have to choose a Bible verse. Any pleasant thought or phrase or even a word will do. I recommend a Bible verse, but the principle of meditation can be applied to other brief, true phrases as well.

To meditate, you first need to find a comfortable, quiet place that is as free from distraction as possible. For many people, the only time a situation like that is possible is after the lights are out and everyone is in bed. After meditation is learned and practicing it becomes second nature, you will be able to successfully meditate for brief periods of time even in the midst of noise, but for the beginner this is seldom possible. For the novice, freedom from distraction and comfort are prerequisites.

Once you have chosen your quiet place, you need to choose the subject of your meditation. It should be meaningful to you, personally, and familiar enough to be repeated without reading. For instance, many people know the first line of Psalm 23: *"The Lord is my shepherd. I shall not want."* This simple phrase would be a good choice, and we will use it in our example.

To meditate on Psalm 23:1, you would slowly speak and think about each word, slowly repeating them over and over again. The purpose of this slow repetition is to give each word its full depth of meaning and to allow that meaning to touch our emotions. Often, the chosen phrase is repeated while slowly accenting different words. For instance: "The **Lord**" . . . **"The Lord** is" . . . "**Is**" . . . "The Lord is my **shepherd**" . . . "**Shepherd**" . . . "The Lord is **my** shepherd." All of these repetitions should be very slow and relaxed.

Slow repetition may feel very awkward and uncomfortable at first. You may feel the internal urge to race on to the end of the sentence. During meditation it is common to find other thoughts interfering and flashing through the brain. When this happens— and it will—don't fight the rapid thoughts and don't beat up on yourself because you can't make your brain cooperate.

Simply let the thought pass through the mind and return to your slow repetition. During meditation, interfering thoughts are simply ignored as unimportant.

## Meditating on Nature

The Bible instructs us to meditate on the works of God. A beautiful field of flowers or mountain or riverbank are all works of God. We can meditate on any thing that we enjoy and that provides us with a sense of rest.

During this type of meditation, the imagination is used to paint pictures on the canvas of the mind. The pictures can be of places you have actually been, or a place you saw in a book. The only requirement is that the pictures give you a feeling of peace. As you meditate, you will pause and dwell and move through the pictures in your mind.

Consider the various smells that would likely be associated with this place. The colors. The sounds. In your mind, move through the picture and "look" around you. The more you look in different directions with your mind's eye the more detailed and real the picture will likely become. This type of meditation is not unbiblical nor the exclusive domain of New Age thinking. It is meditating on the works of God as we have been told to do, and it can go a long way toward slowing down our racing mind.

## Meditating on God

We are also told that we should meditate on God, Himself. One way this can be done is by dwelling on the names of God. There are fifteen of the Hebrew names for God listed in Appendix II. Scripture references are given for each name.

To meditate on a name for God, slowly repeat the name and dwell on its meaning. Perhaps you could even recall how that particular meaning has been applicable in your personal life and how you felt at the time. Just remember that meditation is not study. You will not have books open. You will not be cross referencing. Instead, you will be quietly feeling. Meditation is a mental discipline of imagery and repetition. It is not a research project.

Many of the qualities of God are abstract. These can be a bit harder to meditate on than word repetition or mental pictures.

But any discipline of quietness can go a long way toward slow-ing down our internal world, reducing stress, and restoring a sense of peace.

## STRESS BUSTER # 7: A GOLDEN SILENCE

Another thing that you might consider is practicing the art of silence. Although silence can be a part of meditation, the practice of silence does not necessarily require the concen-tration needed in meditation. By "practicing silence," I am referring to the reduction of the ever-present noise that sur-rounds us.

The definition of *noise* is "unwanted sound." The word is derived from the Latin word "nausea," meaning seasickness. That may be an apt etymology for a word that can literally deprive you of well being. Remember, stress is the energy that we use to adapt to any demand. That demand can be mental, emotional, or physical. Noise is a mental demand forcing us to use energy to adapt. Even "tuning out" noise takes a certain amount of effort. Noise raises the blood pressure, pulse rate, and adrenalin levels. These measures may be only slightly elevated when the noise is mild, but every elevation eventually take its toll.

Think about the noise in the average home. The washing machine is going, the dryer buzzes, and a blender grinds in the kitchen. The kids come racing through the family room while two adults are trying to hold a conversation, and the constant din of the television fills the air. At night, when things should be peaceful, the neighbor's dog is barking and the phone rings off the hook.

When everything is added together, we have a cacophony of racket that increases our stress and drains our very soul. Most homes are filled to overflowing with sounds that can only be classified as *noise*. Much of this racket is forced upon us. We do not own the barking dog and no one asked the salesman to call at 9 P.M. But a large part of the noise that surrounds us is, unfor-tunately, sought and welcomed as a friend.

I would venture that the first act of the morning in many homes is that of turning on the television. Children stagger to the living room in their pajamas, flip the switch, and "wake up" with cartoons. Adults pass by the set in the kitchen and flip the switch for the news. When the family returns home in the evening, a television is the first item in the home that is touched.

Most children have watched more than 4,000 hours of television by the time they start to school. In our culture, the television is so pervasive that statisticians are now centering research on those who watch *more than six hours a day.* In many homes, the set is turned on when the alarm clock is turned off, and the family falls asleep with late-night shows vibrating in their ears.

Excessive noise is not just in the home. Everywhere we go, sound is around us like a blanket, smothering our minds and refusing to let us breathe. Cars, restaurants, beaches, retail stores, and the mall—all pulsate with a loud beat. Oldie goldies, light rock, jazz, country, show tunes, rap, and hard rock surround us on every side. Sometimes we enjoy it; sometimes we don't. Most often, it is an unavoidable reality that washes over us so consistently we hardly notice anymore that we are drowning.

Sound is a natural and wonderful aspect of life. We would no more want to be totally without sound than we would want to be totally without vision. But the habitual, unrelenting presence of so much sound can add to our stress load. Over time, it can add enough pressure to become the proverbial straw that breaks the camel's back.

Because noise adds to our stress, purposely sitting still in the quietness can have a significant impact toward renewing our peace. This discipline, like other forms of meditation, must be learned slowly. If you are accustomed to noise and suddenly decide that you will spend one hour in total silence, you may find yourself fidgity, distressed, and distracted.

For many people, noise has become such a constant companion it has developed into a kind of mental pacifier, keeping us from addressing our own thoughts and emotions. We face ourselves in the silence and that can be frightening. But when taken in reasonable increments and realistically applied to life, the discipline of silence really can be a golden opportunity for stress reduction.

If your home has been one that constantly runs the television, decide that you will turn it off for two hours each evening. Not possible without withdrawals? Even one hour or thirty minutes would be an improvement. Can't take the total silence? How about substituting low music? Choose any kind of music you like, but keep it low and preferably without words. Can't get other family members to cooperate? Go to a private part of the house and use earplugs if you must.

If we are serious about turning down the noise of our life, there will be a way. A quiet, long bath is highly recommended and almost always possible.

Quiet spots can be found most everywhere, but gardens are very effective. Many office buildings now have small gardens. Some of these are indoors where the weather is always nice. With a little searching and thought, you may find a spot at work that is more or less private and suitable for use during a lunch break. If you are at home, step outside on a balcony or in the yard and listen. Don't talk, don't turn on music, don't read, don't garden, or turn on a machine. Just sit quietly and listen.

Learning to practice silence need not result in major life changes to be effective. However, it would be good to set aside at least fifteen minutes for the exercise. But remember that you can't listen and check your watch at the same time. Understanding quietness and benefiting from its peace requires time. It is important that the exercise not be rushed. You must rest, put the worries of the day aside, and really listen. What you hear in the quietness can be amazing. You might hear your own heart or even a voice that sounds much like the Almighty.

## STRESS BUSTER #8: PRACTICE GRATITUDE

Gratitude is the antithesis of stress. It also does a lot for the primary symptom of burnout, depression. Gratitude also helps relieve anxiety by centering the emotions on current, concrete sensations that are pleasant. In fact, there is little that gratitude can't either cure or at least make better. The problem comes in converting the abstract concept of gratitude into a habitual practice that provides peace.

I learned about the value of gratitude the hard way. When in my mid-twenties, I went through a deep depression that lasted for months. My mind was so foggy and my strength so drained that I would literally forget how to dial a telephone and had trouble remembering which side of the road to drive on. It was in this time of darkness that I remembered a Bible story from childhood that sparked an idea. It was a simple idea, but for me it made all the difference.

Remember the story of David and Goliath? The Philistine, Goliath, was a man of war over eight feet tall. He was well armed and well trained. His opponent, David, was wearing a short tunic and carrying a shepherd's purse. David was scarcely more than a boy, yet he took on the giant without blinking at the odds.

The story begins with the two armies camped on opposite hillsides. A small brook ran in the valley that divided them. Goliath moved out from the rest of the soldiers and stood by the brook shouting insults. A few rocks clattered as David moved quickly down his side of the valley. He paused at the brook and reached his hand into the refreshing water. Five little stones lay waiting for his touch. They were small and common, yet cool and smooth against his skin. Placing four of the stones in the bag, he pulled out his sling and loaded it with the one remaining stone.

"You come to me with a sword, with a spear, and with a javelin. But I come to you in the name of the LORD of hosts," David shouted. Running directly at the enemy, he let the smooth stone fly. The rest, as they say, is history.

As I thought about the story of David and his giant, I noticed some things about his stones that had never occurred to be before. David's stones shared four characteristics: (1) they were naturally occurring, (2) they were small, (3) they felt good to the senses, and (4) they were picked up by David's exercising his will and claiming them as his own.

Following his example, I began to look for things in my life that were natural, small, and good, things that I could voluntarily "pick up." The surprising result was that this simple exercise cured my depression faster than most of my clients improved from taking Prozac!

## The Stones Were Natural

The first characteristic of David's stones was that they occurred naturally. David did not plant them in the brook. All he had to do was notice them. It was observation, not effort, that made the difference.

I had spent months trying to force myself to feel Joy and it's first cousin, Gratitude. I often scolded myself for not being grateful and others were quick to join in the condemnation, sharply reminding me how I "should" feel or how much worse it could be. Why didn't I just "snap out of it?" These *shoulds* and *oughts* only drove me further into a depressive swamp.

I decided to abandon any effort to force myself to feel good things. *Should* and *ought* were to be removed from my vocabulary at least as far as good feelings were concerned. I would accept my feelings as they came. It did not matter if logic shouted that I should feel love or peace or joy or gratitude. If none of these things were present in my heart, I would make no effort to manufacture them.

David's stones were not manufactured by effort. They occurred naturally, through the process of time and chance. David almost stumbled over them.

I would no longer try to manufacture feeling on command, but instead I would become more observant. What was around me in my daily existence? How did I feel about objects, people, sensations, circumstances, and ideas?

## The Stones Were Small

The second characteristic of David's stones was that they were small. As I became more observant of my daily world, I knew that even in my depressed state I occasionally experienced things that

59

were almost pleasant. But these feelings were so small! My sour, dark heart wanted to slap these insignificant feelings away. Tiny pleasures only made my darkness seem worse.

Yet if I were serious about fighting my giant with the sword of gratitude, I had to be willing to accept these tiny pleasures as part of my arsenal of weapons. David's little stones must have looked foolish to Goliath, but in the end it was these little things that mattered. If I were going to fight the giant, I had to be willing to embrace pleasant feelings no matter where I found them and no matter how small they seemed.

Walking through each day loaded down with depression is like trying to move through deep mud with a heavy pack on your back. As I look back now and try to describe what I felt, I imagine myself in the middle of a muggy swamp. I slosh through the muck and grumble about how life is hopeless, then pull branches around me to construct a sloppy lean-to. I crawl inside and curl up in a corner to suck on my thumb of self-pity. In the middle of this misery a butterfly flutters into my shelter and lands on a leaf. My first inclination is to stomp the butterfly out of existence. How dare that thing flit happily around when I am so miserable!

Perhaps the greatest lesson I have learned is that I should never stomp butterflies. They may be insignificant and at first glance even seem irritating, but if we will keep looking and welcome their color and freedom, tiny butterflies can lead us out of the swamp.

## The Stones Were Pleasant

A third characteristic of David's stones was that they provided pleasant sensations. The Bible takes time to note that the stones were smooth to the touch (I Samuel 17:4). Heavy and cool from the brook, they must have felt good in David's hand.

If my "stones" were to be like David's stones, they must not only occur naturally and be valuable even if they were small. They also had to provide me with good feelings.

I began to notice small pleasures that I had enjoyed in the past. Little memories of satisfaction came back to me: the fragrance of a cup of hot cocoa, or cool, clean sheets against my skin when I climbed into bed after a hard day, or morning sunshine on the back of my neck. Smell, touch, taste, even physical movement became part of my joy stones. They were all tiny but effective weapons.

In time I was able to expand to an appreciation of color, music, and relationship. Abstract feelings such as security, peace, and curiosity were next to be enjoyed. Depression was still present but the giant was looking smaller day by day.

### We Voluntarily Pick Up Stones

The last characteristic of David's stones was that they did not reach out for David. He had to reach out and take them. There is an initiative aspect in collecting stones.

It was easy for me to decide that I would look for five stones in each day. But because these feelings had to be real and natural, the task of finding them was far more difficult than one might imagine.

I remember one terrible day when nothing seemed to go right. The depression that had been under the surface for days overwhelmed my soul. I hated my day and my life. I was tempted to condemn myself for not finding pleasure in the big things of life: health, home, and God, but I could not connect with any of that. By the evening I was worn out both emotionally and physically. When the children were at last in bed, I gave in to the tears with an uncontrollable passion. Nothing—absolutely nothing—about my day brought a hint of gladness.

As I cried, I gasped for air and rubbed the palms of my hands cross the top of the desk. For several weeks I had been finding stones each day, but now there was nothing. I sobbed as thought my heart would break. Indeed, I felt as though it had.

I remembered two weeks earlier. I had had the flu at that time and every breath had been very precious. I remembered the long nights when coughing spells ripped at me. It was impossible to breathe through my nose and painful for the air to pass over my raw throat. On that worse night I would have given much to breathe freely and deeply.

My hands passed again across the smooth top of my large, wooden desk. I had spent two years wanting a desk like this. It brought me much joy and satisfaction the day I walked into my large kitchen and found it sitting there, a surprise from my husband. It would be unrealistic to expect the joy I experienced that day to remain forever, but was there any hint of gratitude or pleasantness about touching it at that moment?

Breathing and the feeling of polished wood didn't sound like much. So many of God's other children had so much more! Why should He give to them so freely and not me?

I could feel the blackness drawing me. Why should I continue to fight? Maybe it would be better to simply let the giant win. I thought of my two tiny, tiny stones. Would I accept breathing and touching polished wood as my joy stones for that day, or throw them away and let the darkness take over?

"Lord," I prayed at last, "thank you for cool, refreshing air and the ability to enjoy it. Thank you for texture and touch. I will not deny the darkness and struggle of this day, but neither will I throw away these tiny joys. I will voluntarily embrace them as my own."

### Picking Up Stones

Picking up "stones" is a mental activity that follows you all through the day. Think of it as "background music" that accompanies you everywhere you go. It is listed as a stress buster requiring one to fifteen minutes because it will not only be constantly in the background. It will also require a reminder in the morning and about ten minutes of concentrated time each evening.

The most significant times of the day for anyone are the first ten minutes after waking and the last ten minutes before consciousness fades into sleep. These two bookends set the tone for much that goes on during the rest of the day. For too many families, waking up is a jarring event full of rush and responsibility, and the last conscious thoughts are of planning and worry. This can be changed by the exercise of "picking up" five smooth stones.

To practice this stress buster, put something that reminds you of the day's responsibility on your bedside table. You might want to pick up five real pebbles and tape them to your alarm clock, or place a decorative rock in the bathroom by your toothbrush. It does not matter so much what is done but that *something* is placed where it will trigger your mind to remember the day's assignment. You are on a search to find five small things that occur naturally and give you any sensation at all of peace or pleasure. No matter how tiny the feelings, they are to be embraced like treasures.

Before sleep settles over you at night, mentally review the five stones that were discovered during the day. Try to reconnect with the sensation of goodness that these things gave. If you can't remember a stone or can't reconnect with a pleasant feeling, that is okay. Resist the temptation to condemn yourself. This is not another item on your to-do list. It is a gentle method to encourage more awareness of pleasant sensations.

This chapter has given you three stress busters that will require a small amount of your time each day. Do you need to learn meditation, practice silence or embrace gratitude? Perhaps all of these ideas sound good. If so, resist the temptation to try everything at once. You should NOT select more than one idea from this list. After consideration, it may be that none of these are best for you. Keep reading. Understanding all fifteen ideas and then selecting one idea would be a far better program than choosing several items that end up being dropped after only one or two days' effort.

# CHAPTER 6

# Stress Busters:
# Thirty Minutes to Two Hours

### #9—Take a Break Today
### #10—Progressive Relaxation
### #11—A Peaceful Sweat

If the idea of spending thirty minutes to two hours a day on the project of stress relief seems unrealistic in our get-it-done-yesterday culture, don't let the suggested time frames scare you away. When you consider the serious consequences of unattended stress, a two-hour, daily investment may seem quite reasonable, and the good news is that the time frames for these exercises are estimated daily totals.

You don't have to carve out the entire time in one chunk. Each stress buster can be expanded or limited according to personal schedules and need, but the total investment should be approximately thirty minutes to two hours each day.

Taking a Break, Practicing Silence, and Progressive Relaxation can be done in less than thirty minutes. But if you choose one of those techniques, plan on repeating it more than once during the day. On the other hand, enjoying a Peaceful Sweat could be stretched out to cover more than a couple of hours if you have that luxury. Make the time frame fit your lifestyle, but investing less than a total of thirty minutes a day would probably be ineffective.

## STRESS BUSTER # 9:
## TAKE A BREAK TODAY

Taking planned breaks each day provides the body with "down time." In stress language, this means that the adrenalin level drops to the point of complete rest. This does not necessarily mean total inactivity, but that normal functions are being accomplished without the extra push that adrenalin provides. It is crucial that we put on the breaks many times each day and come to a full rest.

Without these repeated small rest stops, we will quickly begin to deplete our limited adrenalin resources and train our bodies to continually feed on high adrenalin levels. One good way to do this is to plan specific breaks between times of high stress.

No matter what your job or how you spend your days, breaking between major stress points is a vital link to living long and productively. It may be that you need to pack a lunch and take time to rest in a park while eating rather than fighting the crowds at the local lunch counter. Or you may need to take a nap along with your two-year-old while the dishes are allowed to set.

You know your personal schedule and when the busy times hit. Plan on breaking before and after these stress points. If your breaks are ten minutes, take four or six or more of them at regularly planned times each day. If you have time for a half-hour nap, schedule it with the same level of importance as you would any other crucial event. Guard your breaks like a treasure, for without them life can spiral into depression and/or chaos.

It takes time and thought to plan effective breaks, and it takes a certain amount of discipline to implement them, but your effort can be well rewarded. Sometimes, an example of how other busy people have put breaks in their lives can help. Here are three such examples.

## The Counselor

I knew one particular counselor who was not really at home when he first came home. Daddy would arrive and go directly from the car, through the back door into the bedroom, and shut the door. Nobody tried to engage him in conversation, and no one started sharing their day. The whole family knew that Daddy was not home, yet. He took about thirty minutes to himself alone in his room.

During that time he would take off his shoes and put on something comfortable. He would sit in a chair and perhaps browse a magazine or wash his face with a cool cloth. Sometimes he just sat. When thirty minutes had passed, he would take a deep breath, relax his muscles, and step out of the bedroom. At that moment—not before—Daddy was home.

His actions may sound strange, but he felt his thirty-minute habit had preempted many marriage fights and helped to build a solid relationship between himself and the children. He had tried life without the break and found it did not work very well. Without a definite break between his high-stress job and his relationships with his family, the burdens of the day kept spilling over onto others. He snapped when he should have been loving, and he was inattentive when he should have been giving his family his whole mind, not just the leftovers.

After consulting with his wife and informing his children, he implemented the break to help him be the husband and father he wanted to be. Because he never abused his time alone and was fully present with his family once the break was over, his family learned to appreciate the benefits. The children even learned that "quiet time" did not always mean punishment.

## The Single Mother

There is probably no more difficult job in the world than that of being a single parent. I know many mothers who would love to be in the position of the male counselor mentioned earlier. There is no way they can take a half-hour break between work and home. The children must be picked up at day care exactly on time, and the little ones are her responsibility, even through bath time and calls for water during the night.

Yet, because breaks are vitally important, some single parents have found ways to build rest stops into their day. The various methods are as creative as each individual, but the method that Ellen chose is one that I think could serve as an example.

Ellen found a way to slow down and break her day into manageable bite-sized pieces by utilizing the bathroom of her small apartment. She picks the children up on time and brings them home with the best attitude she can manage. This is no small task. She is worn out, and it takes effort to keep her voice cheerful and to pay attention to the constant prattle of two preschoolers. Part of her strength to do this comes from her unshakable faith. Another part comes from the knowledge that her own down time is close at hand.

Once home, she gives each child a snack that was prepared the night before and a drink in a spill-proof cup. Then she pops an approved video into the machine and ducks into the bathroom for fifteen to twenty minutes of uninterrupted peace. During her time alone she may read the mail, plan the evening, or just sit on the tub and enjoy a moment of quiet. That short time span puts a break between her job and the rest of her busy day.

As Ellen was planning her break time, she faced a problem. She knew she needed a break in order to face the many chores required of her each evening, but she also had strong convictions about television and preschoolers. To solve this dilemma, she resolved never to use a video she had not previewed and never let it run more than thirty minutes. Did the children resent this interruption? Yes. However, with practice, they became accustomed to the time limit and look forward to each daily "installment" of the story, much like reading a book one chapter at a time.

Breaks can be short or long and as individual as your personal life. If they are short, you should plan on taking several during the day. A work-at-home mother might plan two, twenty-minute breaks during the week and perhaps one luxurious ninety-minute break each Sunday afternoon. On the days that I devote to writing, I take both small breaks and longer ones. One way I do this is to keep a card game and Christmas carols running on the computer desk top. It helps my productivity to regularly drop the script and open up a game of solitaire or free cell. One round of the cards and a few carols, and my mind is fresh—well, almost fresh—again. Longer breaks of ten to thirty minutes are practiced between every two hours of typing.

## STRESS BUSTER #10:
### PROGRESSIVE RELAXATION

During one of your breaks, you might want to try a round of progressive relaxation. Progressive relaxation has been used for many years as a source of tension relief and to restore an overall sense of well being. The technique is also good for putting oneself back to sleep if wakened during the night or to induce sleep in the first place.

To practice progressive relaxation, you need to lie down where you can be completely comfortable. It is also possible just to sit comfortably in an easy chair, but most find it more relaxing to stretch out. If you are lying down, it is often a good idea to put something under your knees to take the tension off your lower back. Rest for a moment and take a few deep breaths. Once you are comfortable, the actual exercise begins.

The goal of progressive relaxation is to concentrate on one area of the body at a time and tense those muscles while relaxing all the rest of the body. This will take a bit of concentration. You may find yourself forgetting which muscle group you are working on or being distracted by wandering thoughts or household noise. Keep practicing. These mild annoyances will diminish with time.

An example of progressive relaxation would be to begin with the left foot. Tense only the muscles in that foot. The rest of the body is relaxed. After about the count of eight, release the tension. Concentrate on feeling the difference between tension and rest. Imagine the blood flow increasing in that foot when the tension is released.

Next, move up the leg and tense everything from the knee down. The left knee, calf, and foot are all pulled as tightly as possible while all other muscles remain relaxed. Wait a moment, then pull the muscle group you are working even tighter. Release on a count of eight.

Next, tense the muscles from the left hip joint through the knee, calf, and foot. Hold these muscles as tightly as you can while the rest of the body is in a relaxed mode. After a slow count of about eight, release the muscles and again try to deeply feel the difference between tension and relaxation.

Follow the same procedure for the right side. Then, move to the upper limbs. Tense the hand and release. Repeat the same process for the elbow, forearm, and hand. Then, from the shoulder down, make a fist and tense the muscles in that section of the body. Release on a count of eight and always remember to concentrate on the difference between how muscles feel in a tense state and how they feel when relaxed.

Move to the torso. Tense the buttocks and release; then the lower abdomen, upper back, and last, the chest. The neck is next. Tense the back and then the front. Tense the face and then the scalp, pulling your ears as though they were trying to touch each other at the back of your head. For each set of muscles, remember to keep the rest of the body relaxed. Hold whichever group you are concentrating on very tightly, and always release after about the count of eight.

Lastly, tense the lower half of the body from the waist down while leaving the upper body relaxed. Then, tense the upper body and relax the lower. The very last movement will be to tense the entire body, locking every joint and stiffening as though made of stone. Then, relax. It should take about thirty minutes to cover the entire body, completing one round of progressive relaxation.

The direct benefit of progressive relaxation is the release of tension from deep inside the muscle tissue. However, there are also side benefits. The slow, repetitious concentration required by this exercise is very similar to meditation and has some of the same benefits for slowing down brain synaptic firing. Also, after the cycles of tension/release have been practiced enough, the body may use tension as a "signal" to release and relax, thus preventing the stiff back or headache before it begins.

## STRESS BUSTER #11: A PEACEFUL SWEAT

Exercise is an excellent source for controlling stress, but did you know it is also effective against depression? Your body does all kinds of good things for you during exercise, including the release of the brain neurotransmitter serotonin.

Serotonin and its benefits to the body have been known by scientist for a long time. Even grandma knew something about it, although she never gave it a name. You may have heard old-timers remark, "I kept on pushing and got my second wind." Today you will hear the same physical processes talked about by athletes and long-distance runners. Sometimes a runner will feel as though he can't possibly run another step, then suddenly break through and feel as though he could run forever. It would take someone far more skilled in body chemistry than I to explain all the processes going on during a "second wind" or "runner's high," but serotonin is one of the things that makes this phenomenon possible.

Serotonin is one of the natural endorphins that are part of extremely complex chemical processes built into your body that provide energy and feelings of well being. Its production can be encouraged through the use of anti-depressants, but it can also be increased through exercise.

Anyone beginning an exercise program should consult a physician if there is the slightest doubt about personal fitness. However, for most people, a mildly exhilarating routine that raises the heart rate to 120 beats a minute or slightly more is safe and will be enough to encourage your body to manufacture additional serotonin. Generally, a good, fast walk will raise the heart rate to about that level of exertion. If your heart is working at the proper level, you will probably be slightly out of breath but still able to carry on a halting conversation if you are walking with a partner.

It takes about twenty minutes of exercise that raises the heart rate to 120 beats a minute to *start* the body to releasing serotonin. If you want enough serotonin to help address your stress problem, you need to plan on working past that time. I would suggest at least thirty to forty minutes and, if you have the time, working longer can't hurt. There are no hard and fast rules. Each person simply must deal realistically with his or her own schedule and, of course, not get carried away with extreme measures for which the body is not prepared.

## PUTTING IT ALL TOGETHER

The three techniques presented in this chapter are anything but new. They may well be the most common advice given for tension reduction and stress management. But that in no way diminishes their value. These concepts have been *tried* by thousands and proved to *truly* work.

One question that you will likely encounter concerns not the ability of these suggested stress busters to actually reduce your stress, but how to make them a practical, active part of your life, not just concepts on a page. That is why I opened this book with a chapter on choices.

This stress-reduction program is structured to adapt itself to your personality, life demands, and style. Like the very best computer software, the program is 100 percent customizable! You pick the one or two concepts that feel right and tailor them to your lifestyle. Then make a commitment to do them for only one week at a time.

If you still have trouble sticking to your plans, enlist a friend or mate to hold you accountable and set your mind to implement only one day at a time. If you "fall off the wagon" in the morning, begin again that afternoon. If the busy-ness of life has crowded out your good intention for three days, take a breath and start again on the fourth.

The most important change may be one of attitude. Be as kind to yourself and as encouraging with your self-talk as you would be to a friend. If you don't get it perfect, that is okay. Any steps you take are better than no steps at all. My secretary, Patti, has heard these stress lectures several times. She says the one thing that made the most difference in her job and her life was when I told her, "You may as well relax, because I guarantee the day you die, your in-box will still be full."

# CHAPTER 7

# Stress Busters:
# Twenty-Four to Seventy-Two Hours

**#12—Taking a Sabbath**
**#13—Learn How to Sleep**
**#14—The Seventy-Two-Hour Test**

It is always a shock when two people marry and then suddenly become aware of their cultural differences. This is true when the marriage is an obvious crossing of cultural boundaries, but it is also true of the less obvious family cultures that a couple must blend. I was a teenybopper from Southern California who married a good-ole-boy from the country. To say that our cultures clashed was an understatement.

One of these clashes occurred between the new bride and her mother-in-law over what it meant to "rest" on the Sabbath. Sewing had always been a pleasant relaxation for me, but the same activity was classified as "work" by my kindly but offended mother-in-law. Sewing that was done by hand (with the exception of mending) or sewing that was done for decorative purposes was not "work." But if it were done on garments or with a electric machine, it was work—and thus prohibited on the Sabbath. When I took exception to the rule and defended my position with the emotionally based logic of youth, seeds of misunderstanding were planted that sprouted regularly over the next twenty years.

I faced the same problem again as a young mother. Then, my work involved babies and dishes and meals. These could not be put aside for a day of rest. At that point, it was not a religious consideration that motivated me, but weariness. How could the concept of rest be incorporated in a job that had no holidays or vacation? I did not have the foggiest idea.

Even now as a professional with the child-rearing years far behind me, I find the question of rest a perplexing one. I generate ideas for books while sitting in the steam room at the gym and on rare occasions find myself thumbing through a magazine at my office because a client did not show up. Which of these activities is *work* and which is *rest*? Since I am on call for emergencies, I sometimes find my day off interrupted by a deadline or hospital visit. If the problem only took a few hours to solve, should I count it as a day of rest or not?

In an effort to help myself solve these problems, I have set down four criteria for what I believe rest to be. The points have helped my clients think through their obligation to rest. It has helped me make better judgments. Perhaps it will help you, too.

1. **Rest is voluntary.** Even if I am resting because I was told to by my physician, there is a voluntary aspect to any true rest. This is why *rest* and *schedules* are natural enemies. Rest must always be something I freely choose to do, even if that choice is a decision to cooperate with my doctor's orders.

2. **Rest is not pressured.** When I feel compelled to get to the next item on the agenda, I am not engaging in rest. This is true even when the next item is a golf game. If there are feelings of pressure or I find my mind using words like *should, ought,* and *must,* rest has been left behind. It's time to loosen up, redirect, and throw my list to the wind.

3. **Rest is peaceful and gently pleasurable.** Any activity that is chosen as a medium of rest should meet this criterium. However, whether or not any single activity meets this requirement depends very much on individual taste and temperament. Taking the kids to the zoo may fall into the category of rest, but it may not. It all depends on which kids and which parents. Sewing, cooking, gardening, or washing the car will be rest to one person and work to another. Catching up on correspondence

is work to some and pleasure to another. Don't try to force your brand of rest on others, and don't let them dictate to you.

4. ***Rest is open to change.*** This is the acid test of rest. It is good to plan a time of rest, but if those plans don't develop, can you easily yield to change? There may be a temporary disappointment or mild irritation, but if the goal really was to rest, a change in plans will not mean defeat. You can still rest. You simply choose another activity and "Hang Loose!"

It is vitally important that we know when we are resting and when we are not, because it is easy to fool ourselves. There was a time when one day of rest each week was mandated by social norms or religious considerations. In modern times, this is seldom true.

## STRESS BUSTER #12: TAKING A SABBATH

Although individual bodies and individual levels of stress damage will vary, there are some markers that are important for most people. Two of these are found at twenty-four hours and seventy-two hours. We will discuss the seventy-two-hour marker later in this chapter, but for now let's look at the twenty-four-hour marker and why it is important.

Observing one day a week as a time of rest may not only provide a time of rejuvenation, but also may serve as a weekly checkup for how deeply fatigue has settled into your bodily systems during the proceeding six days. If our bodies have not yet crossed the line into adrenalin addiction, it will generally take about twenty-four hours for us to get a feel for how tired we really are deep inside. If after a twenty-four-hour rest you find yourself refreshed and ready to go back to work, your adrenalin health is probably okay. On the other hand, if at the end of twenty-four hours you find yourself more fatigued than ever, it might be time to see a physician and reevaluate your lifestyle.

A special time that is set aside for rest is often called a Sabbath. This is often done because of religious considerations, but you don't have to have religious convictions to appreciate the wisdom of taking one day a week to rest. Biology alone will supply enough evidence.

The word *Sabbath* has a long etymology through many languages, including Latin and Greek, but the earliest root appears to be from the Hebrew word *sabat,* which means *to rest.* Whether it is a one-year *sabbatical* taken by a college professor in order to study insects, or a *Sabbath* day taken by someone for religious reflection, *resting* from normal duties is what *Sabbath* is all about.

There was a time when a Sabbath rest was written into the law. These so-called *Blue Laws* have been a part of jurisprudence from colonial days to the latest challenge to them in the U.S. Supreme Court in 1979. We can't be sure exactly how the term *Blue Laws* came to be, but they reputedly were printed on blue paper in the American colony of New Haven. In 1624 this colony had a total of forty-five such laws, and somehow the name of "blue law" just stuck. The concept of Blue Laws is controversial and the term has become so broadly based that it has lost most of its religious meaning. However, specified times of rest—whether culturally mandated or legally required—can still be found, even though they are fading fast.

I was a young teen in the 1950s, and I remember my curiosity about the stores in our small town being closed between noon and 3 P.M. on the Friday before Easter.[1] This appeared to be more of a cultural mandate than a legal one, but I was never sure of that. I have no idea when that custom faded away. I just noticed one year that it was gone and no one seemed to know why.

As I moved through the sixties and on into the eighties, the years were spent raising a family. As the children grew, so did the number and variety of business establishments that remained open on Sunday. I can remember one Sunday when a child was sick and my being very worried as to whether the grocery store could legally sell me a thermometer.

Now, as a grandmother living in a huge metropolis, the traffic never ceases and the cash registers jingle seven days a week. Other than the fact that car dealerships are closed on Sunday and you can't buy liquor until noon, there is little difference between what was once called the Sabbath and any other day of the week. Many churches have services on days other than Sunday. My own church is so crowded that I, along with a thousand others, attend on Friday night.

Laws and cultural norms have changed, but biology has not. Whether for religious reasons or legal obedience or simply because one is weary of the rat race, setting aside one day each week for rest is still a good idea. Exactly when this time should be set aside, what restrictions should be applied to daily activities, and how to train ourselves to consistently observe the time is another matter. It seems logical to me that one place to look for some general guidelines and how-to would be the Hebrew scriptures from which the word *Sabbath* derives its root.

## THE BIBLICAL CALENDAR

When I first began studying stress, it grew more from a need to restore my own health than from idle curiosity. And, because of my Christian roots and years as a Bible teacher, it was natural that one of the places I looked for instruction was the Bible on my dresser. I was curious about what the Bible had to say about stress and what pattern of life it might recommend. What I found was a bit surprising.

For readers who are also of a Christian persuasion, I have included some of my study in Chapter 8 and Appendix II, but anyone can benefit from understanding the Old Testament calendar as recorded in Genesis and repeated in Deuteronomy. In this calendar, rest was not just considered a good idea, but a direct command from God.

Most people are aware that one of the Ten Commandments involved instructions to rest. "Six days you shall labor and do all your work, but the seventh day is the Sabbath of the LORD your God. In it you shall do no work: you, nor your son, nor your daughter, nor your manservant, nor your maidservant, nor your cattle, nor the stranger who is within your gates." (Exodus 20:9-10 NKJ).

However, these were not the only times of commanded rest. There were also special Sabbaths that were called in response to certain situations, and seven calendar days were set aside as holidays. A seven-day party called the Feast of the Tabernacles was also built into the system. When you add it all up, the numbers are quite impressive.

There are twenty-four hours in each day, seven days in each week, fifty-two weeks in each year. Biology dictates that every day humans need eight of the twenty-four hours for sleep. When we multiply eight hours by seven days and fifty-two weeks, it equals 2,920 hours a year spent in bed. If we were following the Old Testament pattern, one day each week would be dedicated to rest. This equals another 832 hours (52 x 16, because 8 hours were previously dedicated for the sleep cycle). There were also seven feast days that would take another 112 hours a year away from the work schedule.

When we add it all up, the nation of Israel was instructed by physical need or special command to rest a total of 3,864 hours each year. Since there are 8,760 hours in an average year, we find that the people were **not** to engage in work at least 44 percent of their lives. This figure does not include any specially called Sabbaths nor the seven-day party of the Feast of the Tabernacles!

I realize that among my readers there are people of various religious persuasions and some of no religion at all. Few, however, would argue that the biblical patterns are of no value, and most would agree that the basic Bible concepts, such as the Ten Commandments, are a good idea. That being the case, it might be beneficial to think back over the past week and measure your current lifestyle against the biblical pattern. Have you spent 75 hours this week resting?

We have already looked at the most commonly known reference to a Sabbath rest by quoting from the Ten Commandments. However, there are two other points that I would like to note. The first point is the importance that the Bible places on a day of rest, and the second is how to make such a day part of our lifestyle.

## Importance of Rest

The importance of a Sabbath rest can be seen in Exodus 34:21. In this chapter, Moses was speaking for God and restating what some of His expectations of the people would be. God's instructions were, *"In plowing time and in harvest you shall rest."* Earlier, in Exodus 20:8-11, we are told more of *why* the people should rest on the Sabbath and *how broadly* the law was to be applied. In this section, we find the practical considerations of work obligations and how these should be balanced against a command to rest. The Israelites were basically herdsman and farmers. Items filling their "in box" and "deadlines" for the work were dictated by the seasons and the weather.

You almost have to be a farmer to understand the time-critical nature of plowing and harvest. When the spring rains have stopped and the soil is dry enough to plow, getting the seed in ground on time will determine the quality of the crop for the entire year. It is nothing unusual for tractors to roll all night and bleary-eyed farm hands to watch the sunrise from behind a steering wheel.

On the small farm run by my husband's family, members took turns keeping the land rolling when it was time to get the cotton seed in the ground. Daddy took the night shift, and the older boys plowed before school while Daddy ate breakfast then he went back to work the plow until mid-morning. Mama did the chores and got an early lunch, then plowed all afternoon until the boys where home again. The boys took the wheel until supper was ready. Daddy was back on the tractor again plowing under the stars.

Summer brought some relief from the intensity, but a second wave of demanding labor hit again at harvest. For a farmer, timing is supremely crucial. Whether a crop is gathered in the morning or the afternoon can make the difference between a crop that is put in the barn and one that is flattened by a hailstorm, rendering the entire year's work in vain. The deadlines of corporate America are usually not nearly as critical as the deadlines that nature imposes on a farmer. It was in these times of intense work load that God commanded His people to take a day of rest. *"In plowing time and in harvest you shall rest."*

## Creating Lifestyle

Although there were exceptions to the Sabbath laws, normal work pressures were not among them. It is all too easy to let the exceptions become the rule and our well-meaning plans for rest to be lost in the noise of demands. If part of our stress management program is to set aside a day for rest, we must continually be on guard for those "exceptions" that inevitably come along. If we let work pressure be a reason for avoiding rest one week, I can guarantee that it will be easier to allow it to interfere with the next week's rest as well.

The Blue Laws that once forced us to observe times of rest are gone. For the most part, even the cultural norms that encouraged a day of rest have fallen by the wayside. If we are going to have a time of rest, it falls on our individual shoulders to figure out how to do it and discipline ourselves until it becomes a practical reality, not just a nice idea.

If we want a day of rest, it will involve choosing a day, planning ahead, and making a commitment that sticks. This is not easy, but neither is it impossible.

***Choosing a day*** for rest is a highly individual thing at the dawn of the new millennium. If you have cultural or religious roots that would indicate which day of the week to set aside, by all means use them. These would reinforce your resolve and make it easier to stick with the program. But for many of us, which day is to be chosen for rest is not all that clear. Work demands and even worship traditions have changed over the years. For myself, it is easiest to make Friday my day of rest.

I work for a very large church, and as a counselor, my hours are very flexible.[2] Because our congregation is bigger than our church building, we have three identical services: two on Sunday and one on Friday. Because of personal lifestyle and the need to provide evening hours for clients, it is most convenient for me to work a daily schedule of ten-plus hours from Monday through Thursday, rest on Friday, and work as a writer on the weekend. I suspect that very few people would find this schedule either possible or desirable, but it works well for me.

Your first step in making a day of rest part of your stress-relief plan will obviously be to choose a day. That can be a challenge. There will probably be no perfect time that presents itself without problems, but if you honestly search, one day out of seven can be set aside to refresh the body and, hopefully, the soul.

***Planning ahead*** is a vital part of resting for a day. We find scriptural precedent for this in the life of Jesus when He told His disciples, "Come aside by yourselves to a deserted place and rest a while."[3] Jesus' ministry was growing to such an extent that people's coming and going were making it impossible for them to even eat. In addition, John the Baptist had just been killed and tensions were mounting daily. It was time for a rest. They all needed a way to get away from the crowds and recharge for what lay ahead. Jesus chose a place and made plans. He didn't just wait for the crowds to naturally thin or assume that a less stressful time would evolve all by itself. Rest was directed and steps were taken to make it happen.

This same purposeful thought and planning can be seen in the way Israel was directed to observe the Old Testament Sabbath. Under the direction of Moses, a certain amount of food was to be collected each day for the provision of every family, but on the sixth day double the amount was to be laid aside so that no work would have to be done on the day designated for rest.[4]

A day of rest is worth planning for. This may include planning for such necessary work as meals and laundry. I know several families that find it easiest to take their day of rest from Saturday when the sun sets to sunset on Sunday evening. This schedule allows for the necessary activities, such as shopping and other chores, to be done from the end of the work week on Friday through most of Saturday. On Saturday night, a light meal is served and all work stops. No laundry, no cleaning, no office work, no homework for the children, and in some families, no television. Sunday is a day of worship and rest. Even meals have been planned ahead, and a Sunday afternoon nap is the best sleep of the week. On Sunday evening at sunset, work begins again and preparations are made for work and school.

## STRESS BUSTER #13: LEARN HOW TO SLEEP

A large part of our resting time should be spent in sleep. Most people need to spend at least one-third of their lives in slumber land. However, we busy, important, high-pressured people have tried to ignore these biological facts. We invent electric lights and twenty-four-hour television networks and shift work. We push the body, call it progress, and brag about how much we can get done in a day. Sleep is a great stress buster, but before we can implement this technique we first have to be convinced of its importance.

Most of us know that a little more sleep would be nice and might help us face the days, but unless we are thoroughly and completely convinced that sufficient sleep is vital, getting more of it can easily slip into that vast category of things we intended to do but never got around to. Understanding a little more about sleep can become the catalyst that motivates us to put aside our schedules and take the subject seriously.

Did you know that only higher mammals sleep? Other animals, such as birds, rest, but they do not experience the shifting brain wave patterns that we classically identify as sleep. Scientists have not unraveled all the mysteries of sleep, but evidence strongly suggest that there is something unique and life preserving that happens while we turn off and tune out from the rest of the world.

For one thing, the brain seems to need sleep to process information gathered during the day and to adequately learn. Long-term memory circuits are probably built during sleep, and while our conscious mind is blissfully unaware of the outside world, the computer between our ears seems to be working on—and solving—daily problems in creative ways.

The old saying that we should "sleep on it" is probably good advice, for while we rest, our brain is more or less jogging in place and ruminating over possible solutions. Morning can bring new insights or an "a-hah!" solution that was not present when we crawled into bed the night before.

During sleep, the brain passes through several levels of consciousness and while the amount of time spent in the various sleep stages changes over time, each stage is important. A newborn may spend half of its sleeping hours in the state most often connected with dreaming, while a senior adult may spend as little as 10 percent of the night in dreamland. Also, the sleep cycle shifts with time. A teenager is prone to be up half the night and wanting to sleep all day while a person past sixty is often yawning by 8:30 P.M. and wide awake at 4 A.M.

Stress impacts sleep in several undesirable ways. In the first place, we simply do not get enough of it because we are so busy attending to other duties. Sleep is regarded as an expendable commodity that would be nice, but is not vital. Stress also accelerates the brain, making it more difficult to unwind for sleep. When stress leads to burnout and depression, the sleep cycles are disturbed. This makes night-waking, sleep-walking, and other nighttime troubles more common. This can form a vicious cycle because a good night's sleep is one way we fight stress. The whole process can become like a snowball rolling down hill. When we are stressed, we don't sleep as well or as long as long as we need to, because our sleep pattern is out of whack our stress is worse!

Scientists have tried at varied times to see what would happen if someone is deprived of sleep. The results have been mixed. Earlier implications were that a person would go crazy—become paranoid, hallucinate—if deprived of sleep, but these findings now appear to be exaggerated. However, lack of sleep definitely slows muscle reaction and robs us of the ability to think clearly. It also lowers the immune system.

Studies indicate that losing three hours of sleep at night can increase our chance of catching a cold the next day by 50 percent if we are exposed. Doing without sleep can encourage or even create depression. However, the primary impact of lost sleep seems to be a general weakening of mental acuity and lower moral resistance. This is why robbing one of sleep is a major weapon in brainwashing procedures and even torture.

Almost all adults require eight hours of sleep each night. While there are exceptions, these are very rare. One research project that has been repeated many times tests how much sleep people need by placing volunteers in a place where there are no clocks and they cannot see any natural light. Participants are given plenty of busy work to do and told to eat when they are hungry, drink when they are dry, and sleep when they feel the need. The results of these studies are almost always identical. Adults will sleep eight to nine hours a night and live on a twenty-five-hour day. An adolescent needs even more sleep than an adult. In fact, a teen may require more sleep than an eight-year-old.

If you decide to incorporate sleep as a technique to help you fight stress, start by counting up the hours you have slept over the past three days. These are not the hours you were in bed, but the actual hours of sleep. Don't count the time you spent tossing before sleep actually came. Don't count the time you were awake during the night. Don't count the time spent in sex. Don't count the time you spent watching television or reading. Don't count the time you were up with the kids. Add *only* those hours that you were actually in some stage of sleep. The total should be around twenty-four.

"Normal" sleep needs do vary slightly among individuals, and the amount of sleep most people require has a tendency to slowly decrease with age. However, these variations are small and you should be careful not to use them as an excuse. One rule of thumb to help you measure the amount of sleep you need is to notice how much you sleep on weekends or vacations. If this varies sharply from your normal routine, you are walking around sleep-deprived. You need to change your sleep habits.

Changing these habits may not be easy. If you have been sleeping too little for months or years, you may find yourself turning and tossing for a few nights. Don't assume that you therefore must be one of those rare individuals who needs less sleep than others. Keep experimenting until you are sure that your needs are less than the world average.

If you get less sleep than you need, don't expect the pattern to change in one night. A good program might be to alter your current times for retiring and rising by about one hour for several days. Then add one more hour to the cycle. Continue until your sleep is back to normal.

By the way, except for acute situations, sleep cannot be "made up." Sleeping ten hours a night on the weekend will not substitute for six-hour nights during the work week. If you are sleeping that much on weekends, you probably need nine or more hours every night.

## STRESS BUSTER #14: THE SEVENTY-TWO-HOUR TEST

Have you ever unexpectedly needed to drive a car with a manual shift when you were accustomed to an automatic? Nothing feels right. The time it takes for the motor to move from first gear to second can seem forever. You were accustomed to a machine that responded to your touch on the accelerator without your having to think about RPMs or feel for that opportune moment when the car was ready for a higher gear.

At first, the process was inconvenient and felt unnatural. But if you continued to drive the manual shift for a while, you may have come to appreciate the feeling of control as you chose the moment when the next level could be smoothly achieved. As a bonus, you may have learned to appreciate the gasoline you saved!

The human body is far more complex than the relatively simple operations of a car engine, but it, too, has various levels in which it functions. We start out in life moving from one level to another on "automatic," never giving much attention to the internal processes. Children run, rest, play, sleep, jump, get frightened, and squeal with excitement in an almost seamless ease.

Adults, however, get stuck in high gear and seldom realize that it has been months or even years since they came to a full, refreshing stop. Often the excessive, continual adrenalin production is such that the adult doesn't even realize how weary and worn the internal machinery is becoming. It is time for us to stop running on automatic and change to the more thoughtful action of deliberate shifting.

Because the body is so complex and our control over the internal processes is indirect, changing our style of shifting can be quite a task. It takes thought and it may seem unnatural at first. However, if we will keep listening to our bodies and working with them, we will eventually get the hang of purposely "shifting" between acceleration and rest. One way to begin this process is by committing to a seventy-two-hour test of the system.

When we are faced with a problem or experience a slight pain, we often "push through" to the other side, where an increased adrenalin supply provides a solution. Sweet success! But as we follow this same procedure day after day, month after month, our bodily systems begin to show the strain. As the strain becomes greater, weariness and pain increase and most often we repeat the strategies that have already proved successful. We push harder and ignore the pain or weariness until it goes away.

In time, the adrenal glands become worn and "stuck" on high. It is not an overstatement to say that we are addicted to adrenalin. Adrenalin is designed to help us through difficult times. It increases energy, decreases pain, and sharpens our minds. Adrenalin makes us feel good. Because we seek those good feelings, it is possible to become addicted to our body's natural adrenalin and never even recognize it.

Adrenalin levels should rise moderately and fall rapidly many times every day. However, when adrenalin addiction is taking hold, this process is disrupted. Adrenalin rises high and dips slightly, but the overall level stays up all day, every day and even remains somewhat elevated during the night. This shift from the normal use to addictive levels of adrenalin recruitment is usually not noticed by the individual, because the body is building a tolerance and it is taking more and more of the substance to achieve less and less relief.

Because these elevated levels mask bodily symptoms, we can live under an illusion of well being. Others may see the damage long before we personally recognize it. Our physician may attribute an illness to stress, or coworkers may accuse us of being unusually irritable, or a mate may remark that we never spend time with them any more. If you suspect that excessive adrenalin recruitment may be a pattern for your life, why not put it to the test? This will take a little time, but it could be well worth the effort.

Our bodies will not register our true level of fatigue until adrenalin levels fall and the mask of well being comes off. Under normal circumstances, a person should be able to feel his or her true level of fatigue thirty minutes to an hour into the rest cycle. However, if adrenalin has been excessively used, it will take longer. Twenty-four hours may be enough if we have not been under continual stress, but if adrenalin addiction has set in, it may take as long as three days for the levels to fall and the degree of true fatigue to become evident. This is why any effort to unmask the body's real state cannot be rushed.

In order to use a period of rest to help you judge whether or not excessive adrenalin recruitment has become a problem, you will need to set aside at least three days for the process. This does not necessarily mean that you will take a vacation. Vacations, as Americans practice them, can be the last place to rest. The kids, the travel, the sightseeing schedule, and the worry over expenses may be anything but conducive to peace. Instead, you will spend three days working at resting. This does not mean that you must stay in bed for three days any more than it means a sightseeing tour. But, it will mean that you intentionally slow down your life and get rid of your Day Timer or Palm Pilot.

Unless you have a *highly* unusual job, you will need to be off work, but you won't be inactive. Each day, follow the criteria for rest that was given earlier in the chapter. Choose activities that are voluntary, mildly pleasurable, and always be open to change. Don't do something foolish, such as going bungee jumping or visiting your brother with whom you are fighting.

Remember, the goal is to let the adrenalin *fall,* not to excite it. Choose activities that keep you occupied, but are not competitive or overly exciting. If you love golf but always end up throwing the clubs or grumbling because you lost, either find something else to do or play alone. Above all, get rid of clock pressure! Don't live by a check-off list or appointment slots!

Learning what rest feels like, learning to take time to make rest a natural part of our lives, and, above all, learning to recognize the danger of adrenal addiction will help us live life, not just endure it.

# CHAPTER 8

# Faith: The Ultimate Answer to Stress

## #15—Know What You Believe and Why You Believe It

This book has offered fourteen ideas for reducing stress and building peace into our lives. These ideas have been tried for generations and proven effective over and over again. However, no book on stress would be complete without an honest look at stress factors that cannot be cured by techniques and positive attitudes. These are stressors created by the hard realities of life that try us to the core.

Some of these realities suddenly blindside us, others come gradually. Some hang on year after year, leaving us drained and hopeless. The stressors may be global realities such as terrorism; national realities such as a stock market crash; family realities such as divorce; or personal realities such as poverty. The fourteen techniques discussed earlier will make even these stressors easier to bear; however, they will not be sufficient to restore complete inner peace.

We need something more if we want to bear these things gracefully and limit as much of their damage to our bodies as reasonably possible. That *something more* is found in a faith that reaches beyond human ability. Faith provides the vital link between a troubled heart and peace even when the world around us is falling apart.

In this book, I have written very openly about my own faith. Some of you have found my openness in line with your own belief system, and some have not. Hopefully, none have found it offensive. But the fact remains that my faith will not help you in your battle against stress and anxiety.

I can teach you how to do a progressive relaxation exercise or give you insights as to how to make daily rest breaks work within your schedule. I can educate you about the effects of adrenalin on the body and give you tools to measure the impact that stress is taking on your health. But I can't give you faith. This vital key for creating internal peace is a quality that each person must develop on his or her own.

Faith is a personal experience, not a skill taught in ten easy steps. Like the personal experiences of love, enthusiasm, patriotism, and sympathy, another person can describe it, debate it, and give examples of it, but to experience faith, something has to come alive inside each individual. This makes my last *stress buster* very different from anything that has been offered thus far. Yet this last idea for breaking the stranglehold of stress is probably the most effective stress buster of all. Faith will work where all other techniques have failed, and it is not afraid of the deep, sometimes tragic realities of life.

## THE PRACTICAL VALUE OF FAITH

It can be easy to think of faith as an ascetic addition to life which, while nice, has no concrete, practical impact on daily life here and now. However, research has demonstrated that this is not true. Hard, statistical data has frequently demonstrated that faith, church attendance, prayer, and other measures of religiosity positively impact our moods, our relationships, and our bodies. Faith makes a difference in all aspects of our lives, and it certainly makes a difference in how we experience stress.

Depression is a strong marker of excessive stress. Because faith has been proven to reduce depression in matched populations, it is evident that people of faith manage stress significantly different from their non-faith counterparts. A study of

451 black Americans found that as the measures of religiosity went up, the likelihood of depression went down. The same was true of 2,956 individuals from North Carolina. Those who attended church had a significantly less chance of experiencing depression than a control group who did not. The more often they attended, the lower was the depression rate.

The same statistical results can be seen regardless of sex, lifestyle, or age. When 760 women living on farms were examined, those who attended church as little as once a month had significantly less anxiety and depression than those who did not. Among 1,011 veterans, those who reported that religion was important to them had half the depression rates of those who did not. And in a major longitudinal study of 624 Mexican-American families that spanned three generations, there was significantly less depression among those who valued faith and practiced their religion.

Regardless of Freud's assertion to the contrary, research has repeatedly demonstrated that religion is good for both your mental and physical health. Drug-addiction levels are lower among adolescents who profess faith. Blood-pressure levels of adult males who smoke are lower if they also attend church. There is less disability and higher levels of functioning among those elderly individuals who through the course of their lives have participated in such spiritual disciplines as prayer, church attendance, and religious reading. Being a person of faith can even reduce your recovery rate from surgery by as much as 29 percent.[1]

When we add the antidotal evidence from individuals who tell us how religious exercise has brought them peace to the mounting statistical evidence, it is surprising that people would tackle a stress-management program without examining their faith. Perhaps the following will help you do just that.

## STRESS BUSTER #15: KNOW WHAT YOU BELIEVE AND WHY YOU BELIEVE IT

About five years ago, my mother came to live with me. This proved to be one of the best things that ever happened to either of us. We are both widows and we make a good team. There is no way I could keep the schedule I do without Mom, and she seems to like me pretty well, too.

Mother has always been a great woman of faith. She spends hours each day in prayer and can quote the Bible by the chapter. That is why I was surprised when she announced, "Before I die, I am going to find out what I believe and why I believe it!"

We had been living together for a couple of years. Mom was in her late sixties and with her health slowly improving and her time less pressured, she had become unsatisfied with her spiritual status quo. She wanted to know the roots of various denominations and if their teachings had changed through the years. She wanted to study the Church Fathers and thoroughly understand their writings.[2] She wanted to know more about the development of the English Bible and how the various translations compared. It took a couple of years, but she is now one of the finest church historians I know and one of the few people who have read such works as *Calvin's Institutes of the Christian Religion* cover to cover. Our library abounds with large, old tomes that are well-worn and dog-eared, not just placed on a shelf to impress visitors. And Mom is satisfied with what and why she believes.

Last week we were sharing a rare evening together. New York had been bombed on her seventy-third birthday only a few weeks before. Relatives were ill and dying. Extended family were suffering emotional upheavals. But the mood in our living room was anything but somber.

"You know," Mom said with her characteristic thoughtfulness, "I get very excited about growing older. It is a joy to think that I am nearly through with my journey. I am not sad. I would not want to be in pain, but the idea of going home is so thrilling."

Many psychological measures indicate that the ultimate stress any one faces is the idea of his or her personal death. Whole schools of therapy have been built on the necessity of facing life and death head-on without denial, distortion, or sugar-coating.[3] From Freud to Maslow, the concept of aging and death are seen as the consummate challenge. Yet, my frail, smiling mother could sit in a rocking chair with the pressures of the world and the family all around and confidently talk about death as a hopeful, exciting thing, and then go to sleep in peace. There is something powerful in knowing what you believe and why you believe it. It is a power that will bring peace in the most stressful of circumstances.

I am certainly not the biblical scholar or prayer warrior that my mother is. But I remember having a similar spiritual challenge at a much younger age. I had been raised in church, but that was not enough. I needed to understand for myself why I believed and what I was willing to accept as true about the ultimate issues of life.

My military husband and I had just returned from a tour of duty on Guam. It was the very early seventies and Guam was the B-52 strike base for Vietnam. Students were taking over the administrative offices on college campuses; women were burning their bras; rioting and fires were plaguing most major cities. I worried about my babies growing up in such a world. It was a time of stress.

I did not approach my challenge with the same degree of study as Mom. For one thing, I did not have access to many books, and the children demanded much of my time. But God had given me a good mind, and I spent much time using it. The odyssey started by my observing a tree through the kitchen window.

All the world seemed to be shaking. Every fear that I had ever had in misty nightmares now seem to be coming true in the stark light of day. My belief in God and His care of the world seemed to be a vestige of childhood myth. I was no longer willing to hitchhike on the faith of others and blithely quote bumper-sticker slogans. I needed to know what and why I believed or if I believed in anything beyond myself at all.

As a mother, I would stand at the kitchen sink for hours preparing meals or cleaning, and always in the periphery of my vision there was the old tree. At times, it reminded me of life because of its greenness and thirst for the sunlight. At other times, it reminded me of the emptiness of all things, for I knew its heart was rotting and within a few years it would be gone.

However, the one thing about that tree that I couldn't rationally deny was that it existed. It was real. The world was real. Believing that the world was real and that my perceptions of it could be trusted was the point where my faith started. And because the world was real, I needed to decide how it all came to be. There were only two choices of which I was aware. Either God created the tree or chance and time produced it through the power of survival of the fittest.

I studied what literature I could on both sides of the question, borrowing some books from the library and others from a couple of pastors I knew. In the end, I decided there had to be a Creator. The odds against evolution were just too great, and I felt it would take far more faith to embrace creation by chance and time than to simply believe that a God I could not see put trees on earth. Even though I could not see Him, I could see evidence of Him in His creation.

For the next step, I had to determine if God were distant or actively involved in His creation. Did He wind up the world and walk off, or did He care? Time, study, and experience led me to believe that it was illogical for Him to have created such an intricate thing as life and then abandoned it to its own course.

But if He cared, did He communicate with His creatures? If so, how could I know what that communication was? What written sources could I trust and why? This led to a search comparing the writings of various religions. I found the Bible of my youth had by far the best track record for trustworthiness.

I won't detail any more of my journey. Suffice to say that in the end I found my faith for the second time in my life. The first had been as a child simply because I believed what I was told. This time, my faith rested on a far more firm foundation.[4]

If you decide that knowing what you believe and why should be part of your stress-management program, you might consider the following steps as a guideline.

1. Start by putting what you currently believe in writing. Don't worry if you don't sound like an expert. Just simply state what you believe, no matter how small it may seem. If you feel certain of anything, put it down.

2. Once you know what you currently believe, ask yourself why you accept those things as true. You may have learned from books, or parents, or formal training, or personal experience, or just your own rational thinking. Maybe all of these have influenced you. Once more, commit this to paper.

3. Ask yourself if you are satisfied with those two answers. If you are satisfied with those two answers, stop here. You know what you believe and why. If you are at peace with the answers you have written, accept them. Only move forward with additional steps if and when you become dissatisfied.

4. If you feel your beliefs are unsatisfactory, misty or illogical, decide where you will go for additional information. Whom do you choose to trust? Friends? Books? Personal feelings? The Internet? Experts in the field? Look around you and take this step carefully. Choosing a trusted resource can be intimidating.

5. Once you have chosen a resource, take your time. Answering the most important questions in life can't be rushed.

6. When you feel you have answers that may be satisfying, test them by ordering your life according to what you say you believe. Do you say you believe in prayer? Then pray. Do you say that you believe God will judge individuals? Align your behavior with what you believe pleases Him. Put feet to your faith and actions to your words. Trust that God will lead those who honestly seek.

There are two very fundamental reasons why faith is such an antidote to stress damage. In the first place, if we believe that Someone higher and greater than ourselves has a reasonable plan for the universe, it is easier to rest in the fact that maybe our individual lives also make sense when examined from a Divine viewpoint. The daily things that happen, as well as the more dramatic impacts, can be trusted to fit together with some kind of purpose rather than chaos. This can greatly reduce the pressure we feel.

Second, faith enables us to exercise a choice that would be unavailable without God. When life grinds on us, we can choose to trust that He will one day execute perfect justice and reward us for perseverance. Without knowing what we believe and why, it is very difficult to be freed by these choices of faith.

## THE CHOICE OF FAITH

My heart went out to a young mother who came to my office for help with her feeling of being trapped by life. Her story was both sad and familiar. Her mother and father were divorced and both lived in the same town. They were constantly fighting, even though they had divorced ten years earlier. Family gatherings were an impossibility. If one home were visited first on Christmas Day, the family faced tension and resentment when they went to the other home.

Her husband's parents might have been supportive, but her mother-in-law was in the advanced stages of cancer and seemed constantly to be needing to be taken to the doctor or given other care. There were three children. Two of them were under five and constantly needing attention. The older child needed a different type of attention for he was involved with church and school activities. The budget was always tight, and lately it had been a choice of which bill would be paid and which would be late.

She was trying to work part-time, but she struggled with deep resentment because her husband's way of coping with the pressure was to buy a six-pack and isolate himself in the garage with a hobby, leaving her to manage supper, homework, housekeeping, and the children's bedtime alone.

"There are times when I just want to run away and leave it all!" she said as she broke into gentle sobs.

After a moment of letting the tears work their healing effect, I asked, "Why don't you?"

"Why don't I what?"

"Why don't you run away?"

She looked puzzled. "I couldn't do that!" she protested.

"Of course you could," I said. "You could grab a credit card and charge a plane ticket to the Bahamas on your way home from this appointment."

"What?" She looked at me incredulously. I was supposed to be a *Christian* counselor. What kind of advice was this?

"You could choose to run away. Mothers do it all the time. Quit your job. Divorce your husband. Leave your kids with the next door neighbor, then find a beach somewhere and take a nap."

"I could never do that! My family needs me!"

"Yes, they do." I agreed. "And I am very glad that you have not chosen to do any of those things. But the point is that you *could* have chosen them. You have that ability. I think those would be bad choices, but you could make them."

In a moment, I continued, "You could have made destructive choices, but instead you are choosing to build. You are choosing to do difficult things because you believe them to be good. You love your children, so you are choosing to care for them. You see the needs of your mother-in-law and you are giving help where you can. Your husband is being unfair, but you are being honorable as you yield to help with homework and put a meal on the table alone. I am very glad you have chosen to do these things and I believe that one day you will hear Jesus say, 'Well done, thou good and faithful servant.' Choices exist and you are making some very good ones."

It took a moment for my client to absorb these strange concepts, but once she did, she began to relax a little. As we continued to visit, we found a few things that could be changed and small ways she might reduce the burden she was bearing. A small amount of time could be carved out at mid-morning for a cup of herb tea, and the cross stitch she enjoyed might be taken into the yard during pleasant weather. It was quieter there and it felt good to be alone.

It might be possible to exchange babysitting duties with a neighbor every other weekend, and she could check again to see if any community services were available to help with her mother-in-law. But none of these tiny practical steps would give her the full rest and support she needed. The burdens that remained her responsibility would not go away. Her life was hard and would remain so. However, seeing herself as a choosing adult rather than a trapped rat helped ease the situation slightly.

The deepest freedom for my client came with time as over the next several weeks she began to renew her faith. It had never occurred to her that an internal freedom from the stress that was killing her could be found without her outside circumstances changing significantly. Her husband was still uncaring and unfair, but she released the resentment that had been eating at her. Her parents were angry and continually tried to put her in the middle of their war, but she learned how to say no and avoid being sucked into the vortex of their battle.

As her resentments faded, her mothering improved. Because she was more calm at the core, the children seemed to be a little calmer, too. Spiritual disciplines, like prayer, became more real, and knowing that Someone beyond this earth cared and walked beside her made all the difference.

As each of us faces a world filled with stress, finding a foundation of faith is essential. Grandma and Grandpa knew that. Mother still remembers how at the end of a hard day in the fields Grandpa got out his banjo and sang hymns of faith. My own mother knows that personally as she serves and learns today, and looks forward to tomorrow in a place where sorrow is no more. I know that as I race through the busy days of a professional woman and continually remind myself to practice the resting techniques that I teach others.

All of us have found a faith that believes God is in control and because of Him life has purpose. This is the ultimate reason we can *Hang Loose* in a world that is becoming more uptight all the time.

# Appendix I

In order to practice systematic stress relief, you should choose any two of the following ideas and make a commitment to practice them for one week. It is suggested that at least one of your choices come from the first list of stress techniques that do not require a time commitment. After the first week is completed, make a second commitment of one week.

You may either remain with the techniques you have chosen, or change and choose two others. The third week you will repeat the process. At the end of twenty-one days, the physical damage that stress may be doing to your body should be greatly reduced and your symptoms of distress should be fading as relaxation becomes a habit.

## STRESS BUSTERS: NO TIME REQUIRED

### #1 How Much Am I Paying?

Several times a day conduct an internal check to monitor how much adaptation energy is being spent and what is being bought by that expenditure. A tremendous amount of energy is sometimes spent on unavoidable realities such as traffic jams and little profit is gained by the effort. (page 42)

### #2 Putting on the Brakes

Slowing down such common actions as eating, talking, driving, or moving can serve as a reminder that life is not a sprint but a marathon and must be paced. The time difference between eating slowly and gulping food on the run is not significant, but the stress difference can be substantial. (page 44)

### #3 Practice Body Awareness

The body God gave you is an excellent barometer of stress. Unfortunately, most of us do not listen to the body unless it screams for attention. An awareness of the more subtle signals of stress and a purposeful response of muscle relaxation can head off problems before they become major. (page 46)

### #4 Coming in for a Landing

Grounding is a method of fixed attention that is often used to control anxiety disorders. It involves an intense awareness of immediate stimuli and an appreciation of the now. All worry is caused by living in the future. All regret is caused by living in the past. Focusing on the present can encourage peace. (page 48)

### #5 Musical Notes

Singing is one of the few activities that engages both sides of the brain simultaneously. The deep breathing required in singing automatically signals muscles to relax, and the increased oxygenation of the blood encourages clear thinking and muscle relaxation. (page 50)

## STRESS BUSTERS: ONE TO FIFTEEN MINUTES

### #6 Meditation

Meditation is a technique of focused attention. The Bible tells us to meditate on the works of God, on the word of God, and on God Himself. Meditation can slow down brain waves and reduce blood pressure. It can quickly produce deep relaxation and can be successfully learned by most people. (page 52)

### #7 A Golden Silence

The definition of stress is the energy we use to adapt to any demand. One ever-present demand of our modern life is noise. Purposely reducing noise can reduce stress. Carving our spaces of silence from our jangled, demanding life can be a highly significant step toward restoring internal peace. (page 55)

## # 8 Practice Gratitude

Using the story of David and Goliath as a metaphor, we exert a conscious effort to find five things during the day that are naturally occurring and pleasant. "Picking up" these "stones" is a way to methodologically connect with the pleasure when life has stripped us of joy. (page 57)

## STRESS BUSTERS: THIRTY MINUTES TO TWO HOURS

### #9 Take a Break Today

It is not stress in itself that damages us, but *unrelenting* stress, which can kill any organism. The problem is not the battle. It is our failure to regularly retreat from the front lines that creates trouble. Observing our normal routine and planning times of retreat between peak stress times can help us recharge and prevent damage before it begins. (page 65)

### #10 Progressive Relaxation

A concentrated effort to tense and relax all major muscle groups focusing on one area at a time is called *progressive relaxation*. This type relaxation is not only a great stress reducer, but it can be used as a sleep aid as well. (page 68)

### #11 A Peaceful Sweat

Stress is not only a psychological state but a physical reality as well. A good rule of thumb is that when the mind is tired, rest it by engaging the body in activity. When the body is tired, rest it by engaging the mind. Exercising twenty minutes daily and paying attention to personal food allergies can go a long way toward solving many modern emotional problems, including excessive stress. (page 70)

## STRESS BUSTERS: TWENTY-FOUR TO SEVENTY-TWO HOURS

### #12 Taking a Sabbath

The old-fashioned notion of reserving one twenty-four-hour period each week for rest and reflection has fallen out of popularity in our rushed, modern world. However, the wisdom of this old custom may need to be revived. Current research on stress indicates that we may all need a full twenty-four-hour rest more than we realize. (page 75)

### #13 Learn How to Sleep

We have been rightly called a sleep-deprived nation. Everything from car wrecks to reduced productivity on the job have been directly linked to the amount of sleep an individual had the night before. It is easy to be deeply in need of sleep and yet not be aware of our need. With a little time and practice we can test ourselves to see if sleep deprivation is a part of our problem with stress. (page 82)

### #14 The Seventy-Two-Hour Test

Because elevated levels of adrenalin can give us a false sense of strength, it is very possible to be near exhaustion and not know it. It takes most people about three days (seventy-two hours) for an overworked adrenalin gland to fully adapt to a state of rest. The symptoms we experience at the end of an extended rest are the best markers of how tired we really are. (page 85)

## STRESS BUSTER: CHANGING YOUR LIFESTYLE

### #15 Know What You Believe and Why You Believe It

Life is not easy. Any book on stress would be shortsighted at best and dishonest at worst to pretend that techniques and tips are all it takes to make everyone healthy, wise, and full of peace. There are problems that have no solution and times when pressures are unrelenting. In times like these, the deepest peace can only be found in spiritual answers. (page 91)

# Appendix II

This appendix is provided as a convenience for those who choose meditation as one of their approaches to stress management and would like to utilize something from a Christian perspective. Meditation is commended in the Bible. We are to meditate on God (Psalm 63:6) and His works (Psalm 77:12; 143:5). We are also told to meditate on the word of God (Joshua 1:8; Psalm 119:15).

In the first section, there are enough short verses provided to supply different meditations for each day of the month. The second section contains various names of God with their precise Hebrew meaning and English spelling. Specific verses are quoted indicating where each particular usage can be found. These will supply even the most serious Bible student with much food for thought and times of meditation.

All quotes are from the New King James Bible. The verses are quoted *exactly* as written in this version, including punctuation details. Brackets have been added to clarify pronouns where meanings may be unclear due to having been lifted from the context. Because some verses were originally in poetry form and line length was ignored, readers may find formatting a bit awkward. Ease of reading was sacrificed for the benefit of accuracy.

## The Word on Rest

1. Be anxious for nothing, but in everything by prayer and supplication, with thanksgiving let your request be made known to God. Philippians 4:6

2. In the multitude of my anxieties within me, [God's] comforts delight my soul. Psalm 94:19

3. Be still, and know that I am God. Psalm 46:10

4. Come to Me all you who labor and are heavy laden, and I will give you rest. Matthew 11:28

5. It is vain for you to rise up early, To set up late, To eat the bread of sorrows, For so [God] gives His beloved sleep. Psalm 127: 2

6. I will both lie down in peace, and sleep; For You alone, O LORD, make me dwell in safety. Psalm 4:8

7. . . . . casting all your care upon [God], for He cares for you. I Peter 5:7

8. . . . to be spiritually minded *is* life and peace. Romans 8:6

9. [God's] word has given me life. Psalm 119:15

10. "If you love Me, keep My commandments." John 14:15

11. The LORD *is* my shepherd; I shall not want. Psalm 23:1

12. . . . . the peace of God, which surpasses all understanding, will guard your hearts and minds through Christ Jesus. Philippians 4:7

13. Truly my soul Silently *waits* for God. Psalm 62:1

14. [God] will keep *him* in perfect peace, *Whose* mind is stayed *on You.* Isaiah 26:3

15. . . . wait quietly, For the salvation of the LORD. Lamentations 3:26

16. He [Jesus] *is* our peace, Ephesians 2:14

17. . . . be clothed with humility, for *"God resist the proud, But gives grace to the humble."* I Peter 5:5b

18. Blessed *are* the peacemakers, For they shall be called sons of God. Matthew 5:9

19. "Let not your heart be troubled, neither let it be afraid." John 14:27b

20. The work of the righteousness is peace. Isaiah 32:17a

21. . . . the effect of righteousness is quietness and assurance forever. Isaiah 32: 17b

22. . . . forgetting those things which are behind . . . I press toward the goal . . . of the upward call of God. Philippians 3:13-14

23. [God] *is* my defense; I shall not be greatly moved. Psalm 62:2b

24. "I [Jesus] have come that they may have life." John 10:10

25. . . . we have peace with God through our Lord Jesus Christ. Romans 5:1

26. . . . those who wait on the LORD Shall renew *their* strength. Isaiah 40:31

27. . . . my God shall supply all your needs according to His riches in glory by Christ Jesus. Philippians 4:19

28. You are the salt of the earth. Matthew 5:13b

29. When my heart is overwhelmed; Lead me to the rock that is higher than I. Psalm 61:2b

30. "Let not your heart be troubled; you believe in God, believe also in Me [Jesus]." John 14:1

31. "Peace I leave with you, My peace I give you;" John 14:27a

## Names of God

*Elohim*: The Creator: "In the beginning God [Elohim] created the heavens and the earth." Genesis 1:1

*El Elyon*: The God Most High: "I have sword to the LORD God Most High [El Elyon], possessor of heaven and earth. Genesis 14:22

*El Roi*: The God Who Sees: "She called the name of the LORD who spoke to her; 'Thou art a God who sees,'[El Roi]. Genesis 16:13-14

*El Shaddai*: The All-Sufficient One: "'I am God Almighty [El Shaddai]; walk before Me, and be blameless." Genesis 17:1

*Adonai*: The Lord: " 'Do not fear, Abram, I am a shield to you; your reward shall be very great.' And Abram said, 'O Lord [Adonai] God [Jehovah] what wilt thou give me?" Genesis 15:1-2

*Jehovah*: The Self-Existent One: "Thus you shall say to the sons of Israel, 'The LORD [Jehovah], the God of Jacob, has sent me to you.' This is my name forever and this is My memorial-name to all generations." Exodus 3:14

*Jehovah-jireh*: The Lord Will Provide: "And Abraham called the name of that place The LORD Will Provide [Jehovah-jireh], as it is said to this day, 'In the mount of the LORD it will be provided." Genesis 22:14

*Jehovah-rapha*: The Lord Who Heals: "I, the LORD am your healer [Jehovah-rapha]. Exodus 22:26

*Jehovah-nissi*: The Lord My Banner: "And Moses built an altar; and named it The LORD is my Banner [Jehovah-nissi]." Exodus 17:16

*Jehovah-mekoddishkem*: The Lord Who Sanctifies You: "And the LORD spoke to Moses, saying . . . 'You shall surely observe My Sabbaths; for this is a sign between Me and you throughout your generations, that you may know that I am [Jehovah-mekoddishkem] the LORD who sanctifies you." Exodus 31:12-13

*Jehovah-shalom*: The Lord Is Peace: "Then Gideon built an altar there to the LORD and named it [Jehovah-shalom] The LORD is Peace." Judges 6:24

*Jehovah-sabaoth*: The Lord of Host: "The LORD of host [Jehovah-Sabaath] is with us; the God of Jacob is our stronghold." Psalm 46:7

*Jehovah-raah*: The Lord My Shepherd: "The LORD is my shepherd [Jehovah-raah], I shall not want." Psalm 223:1

*Jehovah-tsidkenu*: The Lord Our Righteousness: ". . . and this is His name by which He will be called, 'The LORD our righteousness' [Jehovah-tsidkenu]." Jeremiah 23:6

*Jehova-shammah*: The Lord Is There: "The city [New Jerusalem or heaven] shall be 18,000 cubits round about; and the name of the city from that day shall be, '[Jehovah-shammah] the LORD is there.'" Ezekiel 48:35

# Notes

**Chapter 1**

1. Hans Selye, *The Stress of Life* (New York: McGraw-Hill, 1976).

2. Readers who are interested in the rather complex details of Hans' experiments may pick up a copy of *The Stress of Life*. This work, which was first published in 1956, would become Selye's classical contribution to the medical field and make him famous. It is still available in major bookstores and can be understood by most interested laymen.

3. Yes, a rat can be psychologically stressed. One way to accomplish this is through restricting his movements. Rats are somewhat like humans. When their choices are limited and they are prevented from doing what they want, they get rather angry about the situation.

4. Knowledge of the problem has slowly increased, but an entire cluster of names, symptoms and debatable causes continue to swirl around this subject. Some of the most common terms are fibermyalgia, chronic fatigue, and adrenal exhaustion.

5. Oxford Graduate School in Dayton Tennessee, is a small school built on a combination of the American and English systems of education. It is affiliated with Oxford in England, but not part of the Oxford system.

6. "Peace I leave with you; my peace I give you. I do not give to you as the world gives. Do not let your hearts be troubled and do not be afraid." John 14:27 NIV.

**Chapter 2**

1. Statistics taken from the seminar Biochemistry of the Mind, Body and Emotion, sponsored by The Institute for Professional Growth, 2001.

2. The adrenal is a rather small, multi-layered gland located just above the kidneys. It produces many things, including several steroid hormones and epinephrine. Epinephrine is also called adrenalin. This it the term we will use most often.

3. Archibald D. Hart, *The Hidden Link Between Adrenalin and Stress* (Dallas: Word Publishing, 1991).

**Chapter 3**

1. In all mammals, the stress triad is the thymus/lymph node system, stomach, and adrenal glands.

**Chapter 4**

1. All client names used in this book have been changed and some identifying circumstances altered to protect client confidentiality.

**Chapter 7**

1. This tradition has almost vanished from the American culture. It was once a sign of piety and represented respect for the hours of darkness that enveloped the earth when Jesus was crucified.

2. Fellowship Bible Church North, Plano, TX/Center for Christian Care, 1710 Gateway, Richardson, TX 75080.

3. Mark 6:30-32.

4. Exodus 16:22-30.

**Chapter 8**

1. All of the statistics and statements in this section are from the report "Faith & Medicine Connection," a compilation of studies published quarterly by National Institute for Healthcare Research, 6110 Executive Blvd., Suite 908, Rockville, MD 20852. Statistics cited were published from Volume 2, Issue I, Fall 1997 through Volume 2, Issue 2, Winter 1998.

2. The term "Church Fathers" is used for a group of men who were first-generation Christians after the death of Christ's apostles.

3. Existential psychology is an example of this.

4. For any reader who is curious, my foundation is a Bible, and the first steps of my personal faith might best be expressed in the following verses: Rom. 3:23; Rom. 6:23; Rom. 5:8; Rom. 10:9-11; John 3:16.